Presidential Wisdom
for Teachers

Presidential Wisdom for Teachers

Learning to Lead from the Commanders-in-Chief

Mark Hoduski

ROWMAN & LITTLEFIELD
Lanham • Boulder • New York • London

Published by Rowman & Littlefield

An imprint of The Rowman & Littlefield Publishing Group, Inc.
4501 Forbes Boulevard, Suite 200, Lanham, Maryland 20706
www.rowman.com

6 Tinworth Street, London SE11 5AL, United Kingdom

Copyright © 2021 by Mark Hoduski

All rights reserved. No part of this book may be reproduced in any form or by any electronic or mechanical means, including information storage and retrieval systems, without written permission from the publisher, except by a reviewer who may quote passages in a review.

British Library Cataloguing in Publication Information Available

Library of Congress Cataloging-in-Publication Data

Names: Hoduski, Mark A. (Mark Alexander), 1962- author.
Title: Presidential wisdom for teachers : learning to lead from the commanders-in-chief / Mark Hoduski.
Description: Lanham : Rowman & Littlefield, [2021] | Includes bibliographical references. | Summary: "This book provides a self-contained lesson using presidential vignettes for daily training or instructional programs"-- Provided by publisher.
Identifiers: LCCN 2021010692 (print) | LCCN 2021010693 (ebook) | ISBN 9781475861228 (cloth) | ISBN 9781475861235 (paperback) | ISBN 9781475861242 (epub)
Subjects: LCSH: Teaching. | Presidents--United States--Study and teaching. | Leadership--Study and teaching.
Classification: LCC LB1025.3 .H63 2021 (print) | LCC LB1025.3 (ebook) | DDC 371.102–dc23
LC record available at https://lccn.loc.gov/2021010692
LC ebook record available at https://lccn.loc.gov/2021010693

Contents

Foreword vii

Preface xi

Acknowledgments xiii

Introduction xv

Chapter 1: George Washington 1

Chapter 2: John Adams 11

Chapter 3: Thomas Jefferson 21

Chapter 4: Abraham Lincoln 31

Chapter 5: Theodore Roosevelt 41

Chapter 6: Herbert Hoover 51

Chapter 7: Franklin Roosevelt 61

Chapter 8: Harry S. Truman 71

Chapter 9: Dwight D. Eisenhower 81

Chapter 10: Ronald Reagan 91

Bibliography 101

Foreword

Small, therefore, can we think of the progress we have made, as long as our admiration for those who have done noble things...does not of itself incite us to imitate them....For it is a special sign of true progress in virtue to love and admire the disposition of those whose deeds we emulate, and to resemble them with a goodwill that ever assigns due honor and praise to them.[1]

More than any book I have read, the book you hold in your hands captures a truth in which teachers dwell: to teach is to be embedded in a genealogy, to step into history as a student of those who have come before us and inspired us, as a teacher of those who will outlive us, and even as a model for those who themselves will teach decades from now.

The joy of returning to thank our own teachers and the joy of encountering our "teaching grandchildren" – the students of our own students: exhilarating. In these moments, we glimpse that we are part of a succession that has passed the light of learning through millennia and that this dynasty of everyday grace will continue when we ourselves have passed into the pages of history.

What makes *Presidential Wisdom* undeniable and indispensable is that it asks us to look directly at these connections. What can we learn from those who have come before us about how we might teach those who follow us? A student and master teacher of American history himself, Hoduski draws on episodes from ten American lives that offer wisdom as well as caution for classroom teachers today. I am struck by many things about this book.

First, I am struck by its accessibility. The early years of teaching especially can be daunting and exhausting, and so many resources given to teachers who want to develop their craft are tedious and soul-crushing cargo loaded onto what feels like an already sinking ship. Unlike these, *Presidential Wisdom* is page-turning, each page pithy, each brief anecdote sketched just fully enough to spark insight, each short set of questions setting off flashes of "Aha!" You can read a page or two and profit, put the book down, and return any time, as I am sure I will do again and again. The book doesn't tell. It *shows*. It dares you to draw your own conclusions.

Master teacher that he is, Hoduski is a master storyteller, and these stories do not disappoint. Like students everywhere, we readers think we are getting away with hearing a good yarn, only to realize that we have been taught a good lesson, one that will stick with us and keep yielding its wisdom over time.

The book's practicality also stands out. Amid a professional literature groaning under the weight of jargon and educational fads, this book instead offers a chance to think about the continuity of our work with that of people who have solved real and staggering problems in the past. It provides real-world ideas about solving the all-too-real challenges that confront teachers each day. Hoduski has been in the classroom, and he has seen what we see. He talks to us the way the best teachers really talk. He has walked the walk. And he is here to help.

Perhaps even more, I am struck by the generosity of this book. The American presidents you will recall here were deeply flawed human beings, as all of us are. They lived in times very much like our own that included heroism and shame, that were shaped by crises for which there were no perfect solutions, that tempted them to solutions that could cause just as many tragedies as were resolved. These presidents pursued a range of policies that offer each of us something to esteem and something to abhor. They most assuredly would have disagreed passionately with each other about many important things. And yet, Hoduski finds in each of them virtues we can admire, emulate, and honor.

As teachers, we also have days when we know we fall short, limitations we strive year in and year out to overcome. We have students who fall short. We have administrators who disappoint us, colleagues who misunderstand us. Eventually, we are all at the mercy of each other's grace. This book has grace to spare.

Early in my career, I had the profound privilege of teaching with "Mr. Ho," as Hoduski's students have always called him with affectionate respect, and I heard from them tales not just of his legendary lessons but also of how his generously high expectations for them and his bedrock commitment to their growth left them with a permanent sense of their own dignity and promise. Do not be surprised if you also remember as you read this book the dignity and promise of *your* work, *your* calling, *your* life.

What I am really saying is that I am struck by the wisdom of this book and of its author. In those early days of my career, Hoduski was my mentor, and decades later, as years have given way to friendship, it is impossible not to consider him still a mentor. Such is the influence of our wisest teachers. We are incited to imitate them as we can, to riff on a score that they have taught us.

Let me tell you a secret you might have guessed as you read this book: the qualities Hoduski invites us to admire and emulate in these ten presidents are qualities that he also "resemble[s]…with goodwill" and has cultivated in his own students. Teaching is a line of succession, and what it passes down through generations is wisdom. This book adds richly to the legacy we will hand off to our own students, and they to theirs long after we have passed into history.

Laura Lucas
Boston

NOTE

1. Plutarch, "How a Man May Be Sensible of His Progress in Virtue," in *Plutarch's Complete Works*, Vol. 2, pages 131-132, New York: T. Y. Crowell & Company, 1909.

Preface

Several years ago, while attending a summer seminar, I had the good fortune to live in one of the rooms on the historic lawn at the heart of the campus of the University of Virginia. The college was part of Thomas Jefferson's vision to create an "academical village" where the very design of the university was calculated to spark a desire for higher learning and draw Americans out of their wilderness of ignorance.

Indeed, many evenings were spent joyfully on the lawn discussing education, history, and philosophy late into the night with fellow educators. This experience is a fond memory, as there are few opportunities to be with people who share a common passion and are eager to discuss educational topics as readily as they would the latest sporting event or movie release.

The desire to re-create an "academical village" for educators, where they too can experience the joy of interacting with colleagues over the best approaches to teaching, is no small part of why I wrote this book.

Another aim of this book is to identify teaching principles that will benefit both the new and the experienced teacher and administrator. Accordingly, I have selected ten United States presidents from the great, near great, and not so great categories, using a series of vignettes from their life experiences to introduce and illustrate both practical and philosophical approaches to learning and teaching. Such brief stories are an excellent gateway to learning, serving to stimulate interest and activate the imagination.

I must confess, the selection of the ten presidents in this book says more about my historical interests than meeting some weighty rationale for their inclusion. And yet, each president serves as a worthy ambassador, guiding the reader to a critical point regarding philosophy, pedagogy, or character, using both their moments of success and their moments of failure to illuminate a point.

From Washington to Reagan, the reader will find a blend of the political and the personal as each presidential profile provides a window into his life and, equally important, an illustrative bridge to education. The importance of character, leadership, and relationships is surprisingly consistent in both worlds, whether as chief executive of the United States or as chief executive of a school or a classroom.

Finally, each lesson ends with a question. With this question comes the hope that, if at least for a moment, the educator can be transported from the wilderness of the classroom to the cool summer evening on the lawn, surrounded by those who care about learning, with the chance to engage others in meaningful discussions of a worthy profession. Here, in this book, I foresee an opportunity for the reader to create an "academical village" at his or her school, where learning and growing as educators is a priority and a joy.

Acknowledgments

Few books can be written without assistance. I would like to thank my daughter Sarah-Marie for providing encouragement, a critical eye, and a variety of editorial additions to the book, and my daughter Natosha for assisting me to cross the finish line.

I would also like to thank Dawn Wilcox, Natalie Marmon, and Brooke Bowlin for encouraging me to speak with my voice and not with academic speak; Cheralea Purcell and her initial encouragement and help; and of course, Kjirsten Abkes for editing the book and being incredibly encouraging. Finally, I would like to thank my wife, who has always been my biggest supporter and, most importantly, my best friend.

Introduction

This book provides over one hundred vignettes from ten different presidents, with each story providing a compact lesson promoting educational and professional growth. Each chapter covers a different president and begins with a brief biographical sketch that introduces the featured president.

Every page provides a self-contained lesson that includes a presidential anecdote, an application for the classroom, and a discussion question. Each chapter concludes with a debriefing exercise to promote further thought, discussion, and application. Administrators, mentors, or teachers can use the book for daily professional development or as part of an in-service program.

The book is also ideal for training education students in the college classroom, for mentoring teachers in an ongoing mentor program at school, or for an individual educator for his or her own personal growth and development. Whatever the setting, it is hoped the reader will enjoy the stories, grow professionally as an educator, and find practical applications for the classroom.

Chapter 1

George Washington

"I am more and more persuaded that Washington, and those in his country who think like him, will become the best political tutors of humankind."—Stanislaw Poniatowski

In height, he was head and shoulders above most men, possibly the best equestrian in the nation, one of America's wealthiest men, a military hero of both the French and Indian War and the American Revolution, a member of the gentry class, a successful Southern planter, a man of great personal courage and charisma, chair of the Constitutional Convention, and an overwhelming choice to be America's first president.

And yet, if one moved past the impressive resume, one would find a man conscious of his flaws. He was cognizant and embarrassed by his educational deficiencies, sharply aware that many doubted his military aptitude, dependent on the wealth of the widow Martha Custis for social advancement, and privately pained that he and Martha could not have children of their own. Part of Washington's heroic stature is owed to his determination to never let his shortcomings keep him from pursuing greatness. He is a noble example for us all.

GUIDING PRINCIPLE

Few men are known for their remarkable character more than George Washington. In an era in which people were well-versed in dictators like Julius Caesar and Oliver Cromwell and their use of military force to arbitrarily rule, Washington confounded the world by humbly abdicating military control to elected officials. It was a feat few expected. Even George III, king of England, commented that if Washington relinquished his command and returned home at the end of the American Revolution, he would "be the greatest man in the world."[1]

Washington did just that. Years later, in a private letter, Washington described the guiding principle that shaped his noteworthy reputation: "With me, it has always been a maxim, rather to let my designs appear from works than by my expression," or as he stated more succinctly at another time, "Deeds, Not Words."[2] He believed that merely claiming to be an honorable man, a good soldier, or an able leader was insufficient. Rather, for him, authenticity was determined by actions.

Washington's guiding principle, "Deeds, Not Words," has practical application for the classroom, too. A teacher who merely promises students fair and consistent rules, exciting lesson plans, or individual concern for each student is not enough. Rather, the effective teacher will do the hard work of enforcing rules, implementing dynamic lesson plans, and making the effort to engage each student in a meaningful way.

Students will only respect a teacher as their instructor when the teacher puts actions behind his or her words. The motto "Deeds, Not Words," is as necessary in the classroom today as it was for George Washington over two hundred years ago. Now is the time to stop merely expressing good intentions and take actions to prove that one's words are sincere.

Question: In what area of teaching could you do a better job of making your deeds match your words?

HEDGEHOG TENACITY

People do not think of George Washington in terms of an animal very often, but some historians have compared America's first president to the formidable spine-covered hedgehog, a creature known for its single-mindedness and tenacity. This hedgehog or resolute nature was often seen in Washington's steadfast focus on settling and developing the West and was likely related to his youthful adventures as a surveyor in the wilds of Virginia and his life-changing frontier military campaigns during the French and Indian War.

Likewise, Washington's temperament was critical in another arena, enabling him to persevere through eight long years of the American Revolution until his exhausted British adversaries withdrew from America in the face of his superior resolve. Whether western expansion or the protracted warfare of the Revolution, Washington was a hedgehog.[3]

Is it ever beneficial for an educator to mirror Washington's hedgehog-like demeanor? How about when a teacher is considering leaving the teaching profession? With an estimated 40 to 50 percent of teachers leaving after just five years in the classroom, a little dose of hedgehog tenacity might be in order.[4]

Yes, teacher pay is sometimes low, conflicts with parents can be disheartening, and the many unexpected and underappreciated hours of grading, writing lesson plans, and doing a multitude of extracurricular responsibilities can be exasperating, but the educator who endures may reap valuable rewards over time.

Just as Washington's tenacity won America the right to begin a new age of self-government, freedom, and westward expansion, the persistent educator who does not quit increases his or her chance to see academically struggling students succeed, directionless pupils find vision and purpose, and, most rewardingly, see young men and women mature to positively impact the lives of others.

Question: What encouragement would you offer a peer thinking about quitting the teaching profession?

OVERCOMING A "DEFECTIVE EDUCATION"

Most people periodically compare themselves with other individuals and are discouraged by their own perceived inadequacies. This issue is often most pronounced during the teenage years. Surprisingly, George Washington, the man known as "First in war, first in peace, and first in the hearts of his countrymen" also struggled with issues of low self-esteem.

Washington frequently voiced his "consciousness of a defective education," having failed to attend college unlike his founding brothers.[5] As Pulitzer Prize–winning author Gordon Wood observed, the resulting insecurity often proved humbling for the proud Washington, producing a reticence to speak in public or before well-educated men. Possibly as distressing to Washington was his heavy reliance on aides to correct his many public and private letters.[6] Regardless, Washington overcame his academic limitations to win a revolution, frame a constitution, and lead a nation.

Is it possible you have a future George Washington in your class, but a shortcoming in reading, writing, public speaking, or some other area is holding the student back from reaching his or her potential? Do you have a student who is more conscious of his or her weaknesses than strengths?

Point him or her to Washington, who although troubled by his imperfect educational background, also recognized that he had gifts and attributes such as leadership, courage, and character that were highly valuable to his peers and to his nation. He knew that with a little assistance, he could be successful.

Struggling students can be successful, too, if they are willing to seek help addressing their weaknesses. Urge such students to choose hard work over excuse-making, and tutoring, additional instruction, and practice over going it alone. Today is a great opportunity to encourage a future Washington to rise above his or her inadequacies and do great things.

Question: What are you doing to help students compensate for their weaknesses so that they can highlight their strengths?

SETTING BOUNDARIES

George Washington reputedly disliked many of the social and ceremonial demands placed on him as president of the United States. One such weekly perfunctory duty that he felt "compelled" to execute was welcoming dignitaries and citizens in a greeting line.[7] His aversion to this presidential obligation was obvious to the public and led to an abundance of criticism.

For instance, Washington was critiqued for his decision to limit the reception of visitors to one day. Others remarked that even when he did receive guests, he was too stiff and formal in his greetings, making him appear vain and unapproachable to certain citizens.

Although clearly bothered by these comments, Washington's response was measured and practical, "To please everybody was impossible; I therefore adopted that line of conduct which combined public advantage with private convenience."[8] Simply stated, Washington met his presidential duties, but he refused to let them become more of a personal burden than necessary.

Teachers experiencing a time-consuming role or facing undue criticism from students and parents should imitate Washington's pragmatic response. To manage time better, get input from a spouse, a boss, or other stakeholders to help prioritize responsibilities such as class time, grading, sponsorship, coaching, family time, attending church, and social and recreational activities. Every two to three months, reevaluate the list to ensure that lesser matters are not crowding out essential priorities.

As for excessive criticism, create an avenue for students and parents to share their frustrations or concerns. When necessary, redirect the disrespectful individual back toward the issue and away from personal attacks. If criticism persists, bring in a third party, such as an administrator, to ensure that negative personal comments are eliminated and the real issues are addressed.

Successful teaching requires properly balancing responsibilities and communicating acceptable limits for criticism. As President Washington observed, setting appropriate expectations and boundaries is necessary so that the professional life is done well but does not overwhelm the private life.

Question: What boundaries have you established regarding your time commitments and the level of criticism you are willing to accept?

PROPER RESOLUTION

In 1789, the postmaster of Baltimore, Mary Katherine Goddard, was fired from her job by the new Postmaster General. Frustrated by what appeared to be an arbitrary and politically motivated decision, Goddard appealed directly to President George Washington to intervene and reinstate her as the head of the Baltimore Post Office.[9]

Goddard eloquently argued in a letter to Washington that she had maintained the office during the Revolution when the work was "necessarily unrewarded," and she had "sustained many [financial] losses." She further noted if she faithfully held the position of postmaster during a "gloomy period when it was worth no person's acceptance, [she] ought surely to be thought worthy of it, when it became more valuable."[10]

Washington's response to her letter was direct and succinct, stating that Congress gave the postmaster General the authority "to appoint his own Deputies" and it was not the president's role to undermine the postmaster's authority. Consequently, Goddard lost her appeal to be reinstated as head of the Baltimore Post Office.[11]

Conflicts between a superior and a subordinate that require mediation, such as between Goddard and the postmaster, often occur in education. Common examples include student-to-student conflicts, teacher-to-student conflicts, and parent-to-teacher conflicts. Washington's model for arbitration provides timely advice for resolving such disputes.

First, it is important to provide a fair hearing where everyone involved can express his or her concerns and work toward a just compromise. For instance, a parent has every right to request that his or her child miss a week of school for a family gathering or a family vacation, while a teacher has every right to ask the child to take special steps to keep pace with his or her classmates by getting missed notes, doing extra practice problems, or turning in certain assignments ahead of time. However, at the end of such discussions, there must be an authority like Washington to resolve challenging disagreements between parties. Thus, if a parent asks to take his or her child out of class for an additional week, the school official might communicate that it is too much missed class time and will result in a deduction of points for the student. Conflicts are inevitable in teaching. Always respond by listening to the parties involved, working toward an acceptable resolution, and, finally, being prepared to make the tough decisions when compromise fails.

Question: How do you balance rival claims fairly?

SETTING EXPECTATIONS

As America's first president, George Washington understood that each executive action he took set a precedent for later presidents. Confronted with the constitutional mandate to seek "the Advice and Consent of the Senate," Washington determined to submit an Indian treaty in person to the Senate for their consultation.

The Senate's raucous debate over the treaty unsettled the dignified Washington, causing him to hurriedly exit the chamber. He never requested the Senate's direct input again, thus establishing a less collegial treaty-making process.[12] Had Washington negotiated explicit boundaries ahead of time, instituting standards for congressional deliberation during presidential visits, a more amiable working relationship between the executive branch and the legislative branch might exist today.

To avoid re-creating Washington's ineffectual encounter before the Senate in the school setting, start meetings by acknowledging that participants often have different methods of achieving objectives and different visions for success. By recognizing these differences, parties can establish shared goals and procedures at the outset of the meeting.

Such a proactive approach creates a mutually safe and positive environment for discussion and feedback. Consequently, the participants are more likely to focus on the issues before them rather than on the process. Today, set a positive precedent for meetings by establishing clear objectives and shared expectations for success.

Question: What are some examples of how administrators, teachers, and students sometimes look at a similar issue differently?

"SURROUNDED BY ABLER MINDS"

George Washington was described as "[a] man of judgment, not of genius."[13] For instance, during the War for Independence, Washington, a sometimes overly aggressive general, benefited from his colleagues' advice to wait for more strategically favorable opportunities to attack. During the Constitutional Convention, Washington again confirmed his discernment by judiciously presiding over a gathering of "demigods," or brilliant men, who created an inspired document that changed the world.

Finally, as president, Washington astutely assembled a celebrated cabinet that included the gifted Thomas Jefferson and the equally exceptional Alexander Hamilton to design and guide his executive actions. During each of these momentous events in American history, Washington made a conscious effort to be "surrounded by abler minds,"[14] a design that produced victory in the field and fashioned a government that has solicited praise through the ages.

Like Washington, educators must recognize they have limits, too. The teacher willing to seek advice and assistance from others is Washington-wise indeed. Starting today, make every effort to find a mentor to guide you through the challenges of teaching, read books that broaden your knowledge beyond your own viewpoint, and attend conferences that will improve your ability to teach subject matter more creatively and with the best techniques available. Students deserve instructors who are men and women of judgment, willing to search out and listen to advice on the best practices of teaching.

Question: What is an example of an abler mind—person, book, conference, website, or the like – that has helped you be a better educator?

THE JUDICIOUS DISCIPLINARIAN

The year 1794 produced one of the greatest crises of Washington's presidency. Western Pennsylvania was aflame as resentful farmers attacked officials enforcing an excise tax on whiskey. The purpose of the tax was to eliminate the postwar national debt from the American Revolution. Farmers feared the added tax would shrink demand for whiskey and, therefore, the purchase of their grain which was necessary for alcohol production.

In response to this threat against their livelihood, thousands of angry farmers rallied outside Pittsburgh, threatening to burn the city as God had destroyed Sodom, with some of the more extreme participants even threatening to use the guillotine on their adversaries. Washington hesitated to use the full force of the nation's military to subdue the insurrection.

He was keenly aware that his own fame had resulted from leading a revolution against an imperious English government that had unjustly imposed taxes on British-American citizens. Consequently, rather than rushing into conflict, Washington carefully consulted his cabinet for the best way to navigate the complex issue. They advised him to pursue a negotiated settlement with the insurrectionaries. Only after thoughtful deliberation failed did Washington resort to force.[15]

Teachers must occasionally deal with insurrections in their classrooms when students are visibly angry about a test or a quiz outcome, a disciplinary issue, or a comment made. Washington's response to the angry and belligerent citizens of Pennsylvania serves as a valuable guide for educators facing similar tensions.

Like Washington, when a teacher faces a challenge to his or her authority, it is a good idea to obtain counsel from a peer, a mentor, or an administrator. Often, such advice provides perspective or clarity and helps determine if there is room for compromise or if there is a need to confront and discipline those involved.

Before acting, be sure to talk to the students individually to fully hear their concerns. Do not address the problem before the whole class, as you risk creating a mob mentality in which emotions, rather than facts, influence the outcome. To mirror the successful Washington approach to conflict: Be measured; seek advice; practice conciliation when possible, but act firmly if the previous approaches fail to resolve the discord.

Question: What steps do you follow when trying to resolve a contentious disciplinary situation?

TRANSFORMATIVE WORDS

Could words win a war? With the American Revolution on the brink of failure, veterans recounted how George Washington often addressed his despairing army as "my brave fellows."[16] In believing his men were brave, and by telling his men they were brave, they became brave.

His simple transformative words moved his men to fight on and achieve a stunning reversal of fortunes at numerous moments during the War for Independence. Several years later, as president, Washington continued the practice of instilling vision in his political contemporaries, praising "the talents, the rectitude, and the patriotism" of the recently established Congress in his first inaugural address.[17] In both instances, Washington saw the value of empowering subordinates with words that sparked an appreciation of the possible, with remarkable results.

Just as Washington's men felt despair during the dark days of the Revolution, there is little question that at any given moment, there are numerous students in your school on the threshold of failure, paralyzed by uncertainty and a lack of confidence in their abilities to succeed.

A teacher's affirmation at such critical moments can be life-altering. Such timely words can empower a student to persevere and overcome even the most daunting of life's obstacles. Students need to know that the teacher sees them as "brave fellows," believes in them, and will stand with them through academic struggles, bad choices, failed relationships, and the difficulties of simply being a teenager. The teacher's words must be transformative.

Question: Washington repeatedly told his men they were brave fellows. What transformative words do your students need to hear from you?

"TUTORS OF HUMANKIND"

The reach of the American Revolution and its most celebrated offspring, George Washington, impacted far more than the American continent. As far away as Eastern Europe, Stanislaw Poniatowski, the last king of Poland, was captivated by the ideals of the Revolution and its renowned champion.

Admiringly, Poniatowski wrote, "I am more and more persuaded that Washington, and those in his country who think like him, will become the best political tutors of humankind."[18] The king valued Washington as a true template of freedom, spending the greater part of his troubled reign trying to imitate him and the natural rights he embodied.

Even today, Washington's historical impact and enduring legacy is pronounced. Likewise, the effect of a quality teacher on his or her students is quite significant. Although teachers may not earn the distinguished epigram "tutors of humankind," their impact on students can last a lifetime.

The lessons and ideas deposited by such instructors, uniquely distilled and matured by each student, will ripple through generations and to settings currently unimagined, preparing future "kings" like businessmen, engineers, scientists, and every variety of occupation to be difference makers. Teachers are the George Washingtons of today. Their Poniatowskis wait to be instructed, encouraged, and envisioned. Today is an opportunity to impart a new life lesson that will tutor humankind.

Question: How does the impact of your teaching extend beyond the classroom?

DEBRIEFING EXERCISE

1. Can you identify one student in your class or school who reminds you of President Washington? What are the similarities?
2. If you had to send a report home to Washington's parents, how would you describe him if he were your student?
3. Which lesson from this chapter would you like to share with a teacher? Administrator? Student? Parents? Why?
4. Which lesson from this chapter do you think a peer would want you to read again? Why?

NOTES

1. Boaz, David. *The Man Who Would Not Be King*. Cato Institute. http://www.cato.org/publications/commentary/man-who-would-not-be-king. 2/20/06, retrieved 9/24/15.

2. Lillback, Peter A., and Newcomb, Jerry. *George Washington's Sacred Fire*, USA: Providence Forum Press, 2006, pages 142-143.

3. Ellis, Joseph J. *Founding Brothers: The Revolutionary Generation*, New York: Vintage Books, A Division of Random House, Inc., 2000, page 134.

4. Strauss, Valerie. Why So Many Teachers Leave—and How to Get Them to Stay, *Washington Post*, June 12, 2015, https://www.washingtonpost.com/news/

answer-sheet/wp/2015/06/12/why-so-many-teachers-leave-and-how-to-get-them-to-stay/, retrieved 10/25/15.

5. Wood, Gordon S. *The Radicalism of the American Revolution*, New York: Vintage Books, A Division of Random House, Inc., 1993, page 199.

6. Ibid.

7. MVLA Publications, by Mary V. Thompson, Research Historian, Mount Vernon Ladies' Association (2003-2010); QUOTES: George Washington's References to God and Religion, Together with Selected References to Death, Eternity, Charity, and Morality #457, page 87 (from GW to his old friend, Dr. David Stuart [the stepfather of Martha Washington's grandchildren], 6/15/1790, *The Writings of George Washington*, 31:53-54). http://www.mountvernon.org/educational-resources/library/digital-collections

8. Ibid.

9. *The Papers of George Washington*: Documents - Introduction. Mary Katherine Goddard to George Washington, 23 December 1789, Baltimore. http://gwpapers.virginia.edu/documents/goddard/index.html

10. Adapted from *The Papers of George Washington, Presidential Series*, W. W. Abbot et al., eds., Vol. 4 (ed. Dorothy Twohig), pages 426–429. Charlottesville: University Press of Virginia, 1993. The original autograph letter addressed to and signed by is located in the Papers of the Continental Congress in the National Archives in Washington, DC, item 78. http://gwpapers.virginia.edu/documents/goddard/index.html

11. The following is adapted from *The Papers of George Washington, Presidential Series*, W. W. Abbot et al., eds., vol. 4, p. 428 (Dorothy Twohig, volume editor), University Press of Virginia (Charlottesville, 1993). http://gwpapers.virginia.edu/documents/goddard/index.html

12. Ellis, Gordon J. *His Excellency: George Washington*, New York: Vintage Books, A Division of Random House, Inc., 2004, pages 194-195.

13. Parker, Theodore. *Historic Americans* Boston: Horace Fuller, 1878, pages 120-121, http://www.archive.org/details/historicamerican00parkiala, contributed by University of California Libraries, retrieved 1/05/12.

14. Ibid.

15. Chernow, Ron. *Washington: A Life*, New York: Penguin Press, 2010, pages 718–721.

16. Brookhiser, Richard. *George Washington on Leadership*, New York: Basic Books, 2008, pages 162-163.

17. Ibid.

18. Zamoyski, Adam. *The Last King of Poland*, Great Britain: A Phoenix Giant Paperback, 1998, pages 316-317.

Chapter 2

John Adams

"I always consider the whole nation as my children, but they have almost all been undutiful to retain me."—John Adams

The comedian Rodney Dangerfield made a career out of the schtick, "I don't get no respect." John Adams often complained in a similar fashion, feeling he was overshadowed by the military heroics of George Washington and the pen of Thomas Jefferson.

Adams's penchant for whining, his blunt manner, and his diminutive and corpulent physique did little to raise his stature. Still, Adams is listed among the pantheon of American greats because he refused to stand in any man's shadow. He elevated his reputation by a principled and courageous legal defense of British soldiers during the pre–Revolutionary period, with compelling discourse as the voice of American independence, by signing the Declaration of Independence, through skilled international diplomacy, by an inspirational love for his wife Abigail, by his able writing of the Massachusetts State Constitution, and by his selection as the second president of the United States. Self-perception aside, Adams became one of the most respected founders in American history. Sorry, Rodney.

A GRIZZLY OF A NAME

In the article "Who's Really Who," the authors amusingly note the difference between John Adams, the president, and John "Grizzly" Adams, the mountain man.[1] Though both names appear next to one another in the *Dictionary of American Biography*, the similarities between the two men clearly end there, with politically active and puritanical John Adams contrasting sharply with the rough, boisterous bear trainer and showman, John "Grizzly" Adams.

Other than the location of their birth places and the alphabetical placement of their names in the biographical dictionary, the two men named Adams lived completely divergent lives. Only a poor historian would fail to note the difference between the famous individuals.

The lesson of President Adams and mountain man Adams should not be lost on educators who teach children from the same family. A good teacher recognizes the difference between siblings and does not falsely assume that a younger brother or sister, simply because he or she shares the same surname, is the same person.

Such a misconception fails to consider the unique personality traits, learning styles, and ambitions that markedly set each person apart. While one child may be a "Grizzly," the other child may be a teddy bear. Educators must remember that similar names do not equate similar people and that each child deserves the chance to distinguish herself or himself in the classroom.

Question: Can you identify (favorable) traits in siblings that make them unique learners?

BREAKING THROUGH ALL OBSTRUCTIONS

John Adams was a voracious reader, especially in his chosen field of law. Nevertheless, the young lawyer was not satisfied with his literary conquests, choosing instead to focus on the two works he had failed to complete. Determinedly he wrote, "These two authors I must get and read over and over again, I will get them, too, and break through, as Mr. Gridley expressed it, all obstructions."[2]

Jeremy Gridley was the attorney general for the province of Massachusetts Bay and an important mentor in Adams's development as a lawyer.[3] He encouraged the young Adams to become a man of fortitude and perseverance in his studies, traits that were critical to Adams's success during the long years of war and through a difficult and trying presidency.

Students often face similar barriers to success as John Adams. At such critical junctures, students need their own "Mr. Gridley" or teacher to challenge and inspire them to break through all obstructions. Every student deserves a breakthrough moment in his or her life, but he or she must be encouraged to work hard and to persevere to achieve such success.

Quality educators inspire students to reach past easy accomplishments and persist until they go beyond the expected. A breakthrough to success is often just an encouraging teacher away. Be the "Mr. Gridley" of today and inspire students not to quit when the learning becomes difficult so that they can be the John Adams of tomorrow.

Question: How are you motivating students to break through difficult areas of study?

COSTLY COURAGE

As 1799 unfolded, America was on the verge of hostilities with France, their former Revolutionary War ally. News that French Foreign Minister Talleyrand had dishonored American envoys by demanding a bribe in exchange for peace sped the two nations toward an undeclared naval war.

The threat was so great George Washington was summoned from retirement to lead America's military. Not incidentally, the rising patriotic war fervor benefited President Adams's Federalist Party and his prospects for reelection. As a declaration of war became a real possibility, Talleyrand unexpectedly changed direction, fearing the escalating crisis might destabilize the French Empire.

Consequently, he encouraged America to send a new envoy to negotiate a peaceful settlement. Adams recognized that such a peace overture was problematic and risked undermining his political party's growing popularity and his own chance at reelection. Regardless of the consequences, he took the courageous step of sending a diplomat to France.[4] To Adams, war for the sake of political opportunism was not an option. His decision averted hostilities and led to the very outcome he feared: the ultimate demise of the Federalist Party and his own political career.

Like President Adams, educators often must make difficult and sometimes personally costly decisions. Assigning a detention to a favorite student, refusing to practice grade inflation to gain favor with students and parents, or giving a D or F that causes an athlete to miss a critical game are all acts of courage akin to John Adams's decision to avert a politically popular war with France.

A willingness to act in the long-term interest of a student, even if it means losing his or her immediate admiration, is a sign of a mature educator. Being courageous is a necessary part of teaching; being Adams-courageous means being willing to risk personal popularity for the sake of achieving a higher goal, your student's well-being.

Question: What action have you taken as an educator that was unpopular but necessary?

EQUALITY IN THE CLASSROOM

The idea of equality captured the imagination of the Revolutionary generation. For six thousand years the central thesis of civilization was that only a few were destined to rule, while all others were destined to serve. America's novel idea that "all men are created equal" seemed to sweep the world's imagination.

However, John Adams, in a private exchange with his son Charles, reminded him that the idea of equality was not new, but part of the ancient decree to "love your neighbor as yourself."[5] He further stressed that Americans were not entitled to be "all equally tall, strong, wise, handsome, active, but equally men . . . the work of the same Artist . . . entitled to the same justice."[6] Essentially, Adams insisted Americans accept and promote the fundamental worth of all people, looking past mere physical traits to the higher standard of treating every person with dignity and respect.

Adams's vision of equality is applicable for today's classroom. A truly caring school provides each student with an equal opportunity to achieve success while discounting less important qualities such as appearance, popularity, or socioeconomic background. Recognizing that each student has inherent value and deserves an equal chance to succeed is one of the greatest means of perpetuating the founding generation's vision of equality.

Teachers have the unique opportunity to communicate to young people that their value goes beyond race, gender, appearance, or skill and is rooted in the intrinsically American belief that all people have worth because they are "the work of the same Artist."

Question: How do you ensure that each student in your classroom or school has an equal opportunity to succeed?

HEARING YOU THINK

Thanks to the preservation of numerous letters between John Adams and his wife, Abigail, their relationship has become an expected part of any discussion regarding the famous statesman. These exchanges, although often affirmations of the love they shared, were also the correspondence of coequal political thinkers grappling together with the weighty problems of birthing a new nation.

In one such conversation, clearly not satisfied with mere written content, Adams prodded his wife to be more explicit in her thoughts, writing, "I want to hear you think, or to see your thoughts."[7] He knew that Abigail's answers would be of greater value if they were fully investigated and understood.

Adams's approach to evaluating a response or a conclusion bears imitating when instructing students. Hearing students think and seeing students' thoughts is critical when assessing their answers or conclusions. Using tools such as debates, word problems, or essays enables students to demonstrate they know more than the answer; they know the reason for the answer.

Good teachers do not merely hope students understand, they create curriculum that insists on thinking that can be assessed. Abigail and John were a great team, working together to advance liberty and freedom. Likewise, by teaming up with students and creating lessons that foster heightened written and verbal dialogue, teachers can help create successful thinkers for this generation.

Question: By what means do students in your class demonstrate that they know more than the basic answer?

MORE THAN A NAME

Today, Americans know George Washington as one of the great presidents of history. However, toward the end of Washington's administration, politically motivated newspapers attacked his ability to manage the country, implying it would be better to be governed by the "talents and science" of Vice President John Adams than by the "mysterious influence of . . . [Washington's] name."[8]

Adams nobly responded that although Washington lacked an "eminent degree . . . in the science of understanding and managing himself and others, of self-control and leadership, the General was gifted as few men in history."[9] Adams understood that Washington should be judged comprehensively and not on a singular deficiency.

Adams's vindication of Washington as a man of consequence seems wholly unnecessary in hindsight, as all but the most prejudiced of historians have recognized his greatness. However, the lesson is still pertinent for the classroom, as the barometer of a successful student is too often reduced to merely whether a student excels by the classic standards of testing and classwork.

Left unmeasured, as in Washington's case, are the often intangible qualities of leadership that make a man or woman achieve great success in his or her postacademic life, even if his or her school career was less than stellar. Adams's recognition of Washington's capacity to lead, despite his lack of educational background, is an excellent model for every educator to consider when appraising a student's ability to succeed. Students need a champion like Adams in their lives, willing to find, nurture, and declare the best qualities and talents found in each child.

Question: How do you measure a student's ability outside of standard classwork?

THE LEGACY

Few decisions a president makes outlive his time in office like the selection of a justice to the Supreme Court. John Adams's selection of Chief Justice John Marshall, during the twilight of his presidency, appears to validate this assessment.

Marshall's influence ultimately spanned the tenures of five presidents, increased the federal government's stature over the states, and galvanized the Supreme Court's authority to determine the Constitution's intent and proper application.[10] Singularly, Chief Justice Marshall's accomplishments cast the Adams presidency in a very favorable light.

Just as the appointment of John Marshall to the Supreme Court broadened Adams's legacy by extending the impact of his presidency, an educator's legacy is more than the sum of his or her immediate service. For instance, when principals and teachers institute successful programs, implement creative and motivational instruction methods, and shape a school's culture to embrace high achievement and character, students are impacted for a lifetime.

Do not underestimate the impact a teacher's instruction, discipline, and advice can have on what a student accomplishes in the future. Such students may carry on principles, acts of service, and knowledge that impacts society for great good. Today's "John Marshalls" need proactive teachers who envision, equip, and provide opportunities for them to be positive change agents for the future.

Question: What specific legacy do you hope your students will continue in the future?

UNCOVERING THE SOURCE

The presidential election between John Adams and Thomas Jefferson had been bitter. Adams lost, leaving him churlish and despondent. Then, in what historian Fawn Brodie calls "an incredible display of pettiness," the newly deposed president slipped out of Washington at 4 a.m., avoiding Jefferson and the inauguration day festivities.[11]

Adams's behavior was inappropriate but, perhaps, understandable. Besides the crushing disappointment of losing the presidency, Adams was deeply grieving the loss of his son Charles. In what would be the last communication between the two titans of the Revolution for the next eleven years, came a plea from Adams.

He asked Jefferson to have "sympathy for a mourning Father" and his overwhelming sorrow. A perturbed President Jefferson, upset by the inauguration slight, as well as several other impolitic actions by Adams, never replied to the former president's anguished request.[12]

Adams's behavior is not new to educators who often must confront students who are impolite, disheartened, and sometimes petty. Every teacher will typically have at least one churlish, despondent, or noncompliant student. The causes for such unwelcome behavior may appear to be obvious, but as in Adams's case, the actions may stem from an unseen source.

A teacher should make every effort to uncover the origin of the student's inappropriate conduct and apply corrective or curative measures to rectify the problem. A good place to start is simply asking a student what is troubling him or her and causing him or her to behave in such an unacceptable manner.

Sometimes it takes more work to resolve the issue and requires involving parents, counselors, or other faculty members. Whereas Jefferson was put off by Adams's actions and was unwilling to grapple with the source of his pettiness, teachers and administrators do not have the luxury of ignoring a troubled student. Although an educator has no guarantee that intervention will help a student, inaction is a sure recipe for continued problems.

Question: What are you doing to discover the source of your most difficult pupil's intemperate behavior?

UNDUTIFUL CHILDREN

John Adams, one of the chief architects of the American Revolution and the form of government that followed, was prone to melancholy reflections, often feeling underappreciated by his countrymen for his years of faithful service and sacrifice.

Toward the end of his life, in a moment of supreme self-pity, he bemoaned, "I always consider the whole nation as my children, but they have almost all been undutiful to me."[13] In contrasting irony to the accuracy of his unhappy statement, Adams is today enshrined among the pantheon of the founders, sharing accolades with Washington, Jefferson, Franklin, and Madison.

Sometimes teachers, worn down by a long and difficult school year, take an Adams-like view of how their students and the students' parents perceive them, convinced that no one appreciates their hard work and many sacrifices. Such a short-term view is often as inaccurate as Adam's assessment of the nation's gratitude toward his own career.

Therefore, teachers must take a long-term view of their vocation, understanding that momentary difficulties and criticisms do not reflect the whole of their careers. To weather the natural ups and downs of the teaching profession, a teacher should build a strong cohort of teaching peers who can provide support and encouragement, maintain a file of positive notes from students and parents to be read when discouraged, and remember that most people do appreciate a teacher's overall service, even if they are temporarily upset about some minor issue. In the end, the teacher who does his or her job well and does not amplify momentary problems will find that most students are grateful for the educator's efforts.

Question: How do you overcome moments of personal discouragement as an educator?

UNTITLED RESPECT

As presiding officer of the Senate, Vice President John Adams worked diligently with his Senate colleagues to recommend a suitable title for the newly elected chief executive, George Washington.

Believing that a grandiose title was necessary to show proper respect for Washington's office, Adams proposed "Elective Excellency" and "Elective Highness" as suitable names.[14] An amused House of Representatives blocked Adams's Senate initiative. They understood the simple designation of "President of the United States" was all the adornment necessary for George Washington, whose life actions merited more respect than any pretentious sounding title.[15]

Sometimes educators share John Adams's misconception that a title automatically earns a person respect. Students are seldom impressed with titles such as teacher or administrator. They are more likely to respect and learn from the teachers who are prepared, caring, passionate, and knowledgeable about their subject matter and to have a high regard for administrators who are consistent, available, and concerned.

Like George Washington, educators earn respect through their actions. As president, Adams eventually discovered that titles are a poor substitute for merit and worked hard to establish his own commendable reputation. Teaching students to respect titles is good; earning respect is even better.

Question: What do you believe are essential actions a teacher or an administrator can take to gain the respect of students or teachers?

DEBRIEFING EXERCISE

1. Which positive leadership attribute of President Adams stood out to you the most? Why?
2. Would you want President Adams to be your teacher? Principal? Student? Why or why not?

3. To make the president a better leader, how would you encourage, instruct, or correct him if he were your student?
4. Which concept from this chapter has the best application for your classroom or school? Why?

NOTES

1. Morgan, Edmund S. *The Genuine Article: A Historian Looks at Early America*, New York: W. W. Norton and Company, 2004, page 275.
2. Bowen, Catherine Drinker. *John Adams and the American Revolution*, Boston: Little, Brown, and Company, 1950, pages 616-617.
3. Ibid.
4. Bailey, Thomas A. *A Diplomatic History of the American People*, New York: F. S. Crofts & Co., 1947, pages 84-87.
5. McCullough, David. *John Adams*, New York: Simon and Schuster, 2001, page 453.
6. Ibid.
7. Grant, James. *John Adams: Party of One*, New York: Farrar, Straus and Giroux, 2005, page 166.
8. Smith, Page. *John Adams*, Volume II: *1784–1826*, Garden City, NY: Doubleday & Company, Inc., 1962, page 909.
9. Ibid.
10. Smith, Jean Edward. *John Marshall: Definer of a Nation*, New York: Henry Holt and Company, 1996, pages 1-2.
11. Brodie, Fawn M. *Thomas Jefferson: An Intimate History*, New York: Norton & Company, Inc., 1974, pages 334-335.
12. Ibid.
13. Peterson, Merrill D. *Adams and Jefferson: A Revolutionary Dialogue*, Oxford: Oxford University Press, 1976, page 95.
14. http://www.si.edu, 2/28/2012, *Collections: The Patriot Papers*, Middle School, Spring 2003, Seattle, http://si-pwebsrch02.si.edu/search?q=cache:aG1y3G5YFZUJ:http://georgewashington.si.edu/kids/pp4m_7.html+john%20adams&output=xml_no_dtd&client=www-si-edu&proxystylesheet=www-si-edu&site=si_all
15. Ibid.

Chapter 3

Thomas Jefferson

"We are not to expect to be translated from despotism to liberty in a feather bed."—Thomas Jefferson

Author of the Declaration of Independence, governor of Virginia, champion of religious liberty, founder of the University of Virginia, sponsor of the Lewis and Clark expedition, inventor, ambassador, the first secretary of state, innovative Southern planter, procurer of the Louisiana Purchase, and the third president of the United States.

Amazingly, this list of achievements does not even adequately illustrate Jefferson's greatness and accomplishments. Nor does it address his penchant for incurring debt, his less than heroic flight from a British patrol during the American Revolution, his secretive and virulent attacks on political opponents, his affair with his slave Sally Hemings, and most infamously his continuation of slavery after declaring "all men are created equal." Nevertheless, fine silver, even when tarnished, is still silver. Such is the case with Thomas Jefferson.

ACTING ON KNOWLEDGE

Thomas Jefferson is undeniably a great man whose accomplishments fill countless books with noteworthy achievements and accolades. Yet, there is one issue for which he is universally censured—slavery.

In a letter to French journalist and abolitionist Brissot de Warville, Jefferson intoned, "You know that nobody wishes more ardently to see an abolition not only of the trade but of the condition of slavery: and certainly, nobody will be more willing to encounter every sacrifice for that object."[1] Historians can identify few Jeffersonian sacrifices on slavery to match his noble sentiments. It was not that Jefferson failed to say the right things on slavery; it was that he failed to act on what he said.

Teachers can help students avoid the folly of Jeffersonian inaction by setting an expectation that students put into practice what they learn. The

Apostle James succinctly expressed the idea: "Do not merely listen to the word, and so deceive yourselves. Do what it says."[2]

Requiring students to act upon the ideas they are exposed to, rather than merely reading or hearing about them, is an essential part of the educational experience. Practical implementation of learning should include discussion, writing, planning, creating, debating, simulating, or any other activity that involves students in analyzing and practicing what they learned.

Essentially, students must set the knowledge they acquire in motion; otherwise, the concepts simply remain words, even as Jefferson's slaves remained captive.

Question: How can you help students practice what they learn?

DESIGNING A PROCESS FOR LEADERSHIP GROWTH

Historian Charles S. Sydnor surmises that the great statesmen of Virginia, such as Thomas Jefferson, were the product of a two-part process that prepared them to be leaders on the national stage. According to this model, the first step toward leadership began as an official in the county court, which provided a "practical education in the school of government."[3]

Here the novice learned from his more seasoned peers such basics as civil and criminal law, administration, and writing tax laws. As the increasingly public figure's experience grew, he advanced to the House of Burgesses, Virginia's legislature.

Here, he developed the art of deliberation and speech-making, mastered the intricacies of the assembly's rules, learned how to write public documents, and sharpened the ability "to see the distant tendency of immediate problems." The training complete, men like Thomas Jefferson moved on to the national scene.[4]

The results of the Virginia leadership development process, which produced leaders like Thomas Jefferson, George Washington, and James Madison, are astounding. Designing classroom practices that mirror such a successful leadership paradigm, while difficult, is not impossible.

A good starting point for imitating the Virginians' success is the introduction of cooperative learning activities that pair students with more advanced peers while requiring them to develop their own critical thinking, speaking, and writing abilities. Obliging students to take these skills and practices and apply them in real-life situations, whether at work, their church, or during a community service project, is the next logical step in the maturation process.

Each of these critical phases allows students to experience moments of failure and growth which are necessary for advancing to the next stage. Every organization, profession, or ministry needs leaders who can manage the ordinary and prepare for the extraordinary; begin preparing students for both today.

Question: What processes are you using for developing leaders?

ENCOURAGING HISTORICAL CURIOSITY

Historical markers dot the highways of America like so many lost shoes easily overlooked as mere clutter. Most Americans give little thought to the humble signs and suffer few pangs of guilt as they pass by, racing to their destination.

But what if they stopped? What treasure of knowledge and long-forgotten adventures might they discover? Thomas Jefferson sagely advised Americans, based on his travels to Europe, how to determine if a place was worthy of investigation, recording, "When you are doubting whether a thing is worth the trouble of going to see, recollect that you will never again be so near it, that you may repent the not having seen it, but can never repent having seen it."[5]

Students unacquainted with the historical anecdotes scattered about the countryside will not feel compelled to investigate them, nor will they feel any need to repent for not having seen them. Jefferson's words of advice remind teachers to nurture in their students a historical curiosity, even for the obscure, that compels them to search for the hidden treasures of life, whether on the roadside, in their communities, or in their local libraries.

Few actions cultivate historical curiosity as much as a good story shared by a teacher of his or her own adventures viewing forgotten places, books, signs, or graves. The first step is to let students know that the treasure is out there and, then, to inspire them to see it.

Question: How are you developing historical curiosity in your students?

EXPOSING STUDENTS TO PEOPLE OF INFLUENCE

Americans know Meriwether Lewis as one half of the dynamic pair of explorers who traversed and mapped the newly acquired Louisiana Purchase. But before this adventure ever occurred, his mentor, Thomas Jefferson, appointed Lewis as his private secretary and arranged for him to meet an array of people who greatly influenced the future adventurer.

Jefferson assured Lewis his appointment as secretary would permit him to "'know and be known to characters of influence in the affairs of our country, and give you the advantage of their wisdom.'"[6]

Over the course of their relationship, Jefferson introduced the prospective trailblazer to leading figures like future president James Madison and his vibrant wife, Dolly; General Dearborn, veteran of the Revolutionary War; poet Joel Barlow; artist Charles Wilson Peale; and author Thomas Paine.[7] The meetings provided Lewis with living testimonies of inspiration and success and afforded him invaluable access and information that shaped and advanced his meteoric career.

What Jefferson did for Lewis, teachers can do for their students by exposing them to an assortment of influential people. Whether community leaders, local entrepreneurs, successful alumni, or other educators, such meetings are beneficial to student growth and development, piquing their curiosity, challenging the dullness of their views, and inspiring them to pursue a higher station. Helping students "know and be known to characters of influence" can open doors and adventures that will impact a student for a lifetime. Be a student's Jefferson and introduce them to men and women of experience, wisdom, and inspiration today.

Question: What "characters of influence" are you exposing your students to?

FORGET THE FLIES

During Thomas Jefferson's latter years, he loved to share a story about the signing of the Declaration of Independence that brought great delight to his audiences. According to the celebrated founder, the staid and dignified image of the signing of the Declaration, often portrayed in the paintings of the era, was quite inaccurate.

In his version, flies, bred in a nearby horse stable, came through the unscreened windows and proved such a nuisance to the signers that the ceremony was completed quickly and with a minimum of pomp.[8] The recollection is a rather humorous and unseemly picture of the famous event, but of course, does not diminish the importance of what was accomplished on that historic date. Regardless of the flies, American freedom was nevertheless born that day.

School years have flies, too. The teaching assignment that fails, the inattentive or disrespectful student, or the tedium of extra duties all reflect the daily minor difficulties of the teaching profession, comparable to swarming, exasperating flies.

Perhaps the lesson to learn from Jefferson is that such small inconveniences should be relegated to humorous anecdotes, while achievements such as witnessing a struggling student go on to graduate and have a productive and a worthy life should be highlighted and cherished. Remember, big successes can happen amid little defeats, so laugh about the flies and keep teaching.

Question: Can you share a funny teaching anecdote filled with flies that still led to an accomplishment?

NO FEATHER BEDS IN TEACHING

In the late eighteenth century, one of the heroes of the American Revolution, the French idealist and patriot-mercenary, the Marquis de Lafayette, returned home to France following the defeat of the British. He hoped to replicate the liberty he helped Americans achieve by winning it for the people of his beloved France.

However, he quickly discovered that the dream could not be easily replicated, as the French government and the French citizens seemed incapable of embracing the American model of revolutionary change. In desperation, he turned to his colleague and friend from the American Revolution, Thomas Jefferson, for advice.

The American statesmen tempered Lafayette's discouragement, writing, "But we are not to expect to be translated from despotism to liberty in a feather bed."[9] Simply stated: change is hard, persevere.

Jefferson's perceptive letter to the Marquis de Lafayette, about the difficulties of transforming a monarchical or statist culture into a free society is applicable for the teacher aspiring to change a culture of low standards and muted expectations in a classroom or a school.

Teaching success, like societies, seldom advances without difficulties. Lafayette appears to have forgotten that the American Revolution took eight long years and was preceded by multiple growing pains including the Stamp Act, the Tea Act, and the Coercive Acts, all events that sharpened American appetites for freedom.

The astute educator understands that success, even with setbacks and obstacles, is still attainable with a willingness to adapt, to grow, and, most of all, to persevere. There are no feather beds in teaching either.

Question: What are some of the most difficult challenges you face in overcoming a culture of low expectations and intransigency?

POWER SHARING

The struggle to throw off the tyranny of Britain was a long and trying experience for Americans. As Thomas Jefferson and the other founders pondered what form of government America should have, they hoped to avoid the construction of a similarly powerful and oppressive British-like institution.

Jefferson's wariness of despotism was evident: "I own, I am not a friend to a very energetic government. It is always oppressive."[10] Jefferson understood the best way to counter government overreach was an informed citizenry.

Such a society tends to be proactive and develop an ability to solve problems, which naturally leads to a decreased need for government action. For Jefferson, an active and educated electorate was necessary to remind the governing authority that its mandate was to serve at the pleasure of the people and not the other way around.

Likewise, just as an informed citizenry is necessary for maintaining a flourishing republic, informed parents are equally essential in helping a struggling student find success. An energetic teacher is always good, but like the overly energetic government, the teacher's actions should not come at the expense of parental involvement.

The creation of a working triad of teacher, student, and parents, with equal responsibility to find and build a positive outcome, is always preferable to a teacher operating alone. Teachers are seldom successful when they simply dictate a remedy for a pupil's struggles without empowering parents to participate in the solution. Good teaching means helping parents become active in the success of their child.

Question: What specific steps do you need to take to better inform and involve your parents in their children's education?

SETTING OBJECTIVES

In preparation for exploring the newly acquired Louisiana Purchase, Jefferson set broad objectives for the expeditionary team assigned to survey the mysterious landscape, such as identifying opportunities for trade, examining soil types for farmers, and observing climatic conditions.

While Jefferson did not personally travel with the expedition, his pre-trip guidance played a pivotal role in its success. Critically, Jefferson sagely allowed Captain Lewis, the commander of the enterprise, great leeway to determine and define the essential details of the trip, such as how to "get the expedition there and back."[11]

Lewis also established the number of men necessary for success, the type of boats best suited for travel on the Missouri River, and the best kinds of equipment and medicines to achieve their ambitious plan to reach the Pacific Ocean.[12] The team of Jefferson and Lewis, each playing his role, attained remarkable success in exploring the new Louisiana territory.

Jefferson's model of setting large objectives while leaving the details to the person most directly involved in carrying out the mission is an ideal method for educators to adapt to their classrooms. By establishing broad objectives for each lesson, students are better equipped to understand where they are going and what they are expected to achieve.

However, requiring students to discern and plan how to independently reach these objectives is critical for developing their intellectual independence. In the end, creating student-explorers means setting a destination for the students to journey toward and then making them responsible for how to get there. Start the journey with students today.

Question: How are you setting broad objectives for your students to reach while challenging them to define and address the specific details necessary to achieve the broader goals?

THE CIVILIZING FORCE

Thomas Jefferson, the educator, was ahead of his time. He understood that education was not solely found in the classroom lecture. For him, multiple learning styles was not merely academic jargon but a vibrant component of the learning experience. His educational philosophy was abundantly clear when he designed the University of Virginia.

As the historian James Fitch notes, Jefferson believed the very buildings should help to instruct the rather unrefined sons of the gentry, both civilizing and spurring them to greatness. By incorporating both "Greek democracy and Roman republicanism" into his architecture, he demonstrated how learning and participation were to be revered like a temple in the ancient world.

Jefferson's architectural lesson also provided inspiration to countless Virginian students by modeling how they were to participate in building a new and successful republic in America.[13] Every day at the university was a visual lesson for students.

Jefferson worked to create an "academical village" or visual educational setting through architecture that promoted learning. Similarly, teachers can arrange classrooms to teach, inspire, and civilize students as purposefully as intended at the University of Virginia.

Posters, prominently displayed quotes, desk arrangements, color schemes, and a host of other creative approaches can help students better visualize and grasp central ideas and themes. Accordingly, imitate Jefferson's passion for sensory learning by incorporating visuals throughout the room, knowing that such actions may inspire students to build a better society for everyone.

Question: How is your classroom a civilizing and inspiring force in the lives of your students?

VOICE OF MODERATION

President Adams faced growing public hostility over the Alien and Sedition Acts he championed. The legislation was designed to deport foreigners seen as a threat to the nation and to silence, through prosecution, any statements deemed harmful or malicious toward the government. Adams feared that France, America's Revolutionary War ally, was now actively undermining the United States's sovereignty by sending French nationals to infiltrate American politics and culture. Thomas Jefferson, Adams's vice president and, ironically, the leader of the political opposition, disagreed.

Unlike Adams, Jefferson was a friend and supporter of all things French and readied a letter that threatened secession unless President Adams disavowed the provocative measures. Jefferson believed the Acts trampled the fundamental American principles of self-government and civil liberty.

Fortunately, Jefferson sought the counsel of the more temperate James Madison, who persuaded Jefferson not to include the radical threat of secession in his correspondence.[14] As a result, an open national breach and a possible civil war was averted.

Every teacher or administrator needs a Madison, or voice of reason, to turn to for counsel. To this end, building relationships with peers or mentors who can be trusted to play the Madisonian role is essential. Whether responding to an irate parent, confronting a difficult student, or resolving a conflict with a peer, having a reliable voice of reason to consult when facing an unsettling issue is invaluable.

A Madison-like figure can help you distinguish between constructive words that bring resolution and emotion-laden words that risk further compounding the problem. Do not forget, even the accomplished Jefferson needed a Madison to prevent him from taking foolish actions. A good teacher finds a Madison-like confidant and listens to him or her.

Question: Who is the voice of moderation in your professional life?

DEBRIEFING EXERCISE

Thomas Jefferson believed architecture could be a civilizing force communicating knowledge beyond a classroom lecture.

Put this idea to the test by . . .

1. Walking around the outside of your school. Be sure to observe all signs, the buildings, the landscaping, colors, etc. What message does your school communicate?

2. Touring classrooms. What do the color schemes, bulletin boards, the way the classes are arranged, the location of the teacher's desk or podium, posters, and so on communicate?
3. Analyzing your classroom or office. What do you wish your class or office communicates to students? What do you think it actually communicates to students?
4. What changes might you make to fashion your class or office into a civilizing force?

NOTES

1. Extract from Thomas Jefferson's letter to Brissot de Warville, in the Papers of Thomas Jefferson Retirement Series Digital Library. www.monticello.org, 6/30/2010.

2. Book of James, in *The Comparative Study Bible, Michigan*: The Zondervan Corporation, 1984, page 3003.

3. Sydnor, Charles S. *Gentlemen Freeholders: Political Practices in Washington's Virginia*, Chapel Hill, NC, 1952), pages 113, 119.

4. Ibid.

5. Extract from Thomas Jefferson's Hints to Americans Traveling in Europe, in the Papers of Thomas Jefferson Retirement Series Digital Library. www.monticello.org, 6/30/2010.

6. Ambrose, Stephan E. *Undaunted Courage*. USA: Simon and Schuster, 1996, pages 63-64.

7. Ibid.

8. Wilstach, Paul. *Patriots off Their Pedestals*, Indianapolis: The Bobbs-Merrill Company, 1927, page 170-171.

9. Mayo, Bernard. *Jefferson Himself: The Personal Narrative of a Many-Sided American*, Charlottesville: The University Press of Virginia 1984, page. 155.

10. Padover, Saul K. *The Complete Jefferson*, New York: Duell, Sloan, and Pearce, Inc., 1943, pages 122-123.

11. Ambrose, *Undaunted Courage*, pages 81-84.

12. Ibid.

13. Fitch, James Marston. The Lawn: America's Greatest Architectural Achievement, *American Heritage Magazine*, Volume 35, Issue 4 (June/July 1984), pages 51, 53, and 55.

14. Simon, James F. *What Kind of Nation: Thomas Jefferson, John Marshall, and the Epic Struggle to Create a United States*, New York: Simon & Schuster, 2002, pages 51, 105-106.

Chapter 4

Abraham Lincoln

"We shall sooner have the fowl by hatching the egg than by smashing it."
—Abraham Lincoln

It was not easy being Abraham Lincoln. His irregular shaped face drew endless critique, with one little girl suggesting he grow a beard to improve his unattractive appearance. The national media was unkind, even referring to him as a baboon. Three out of four of his children died while he was in office, and his wife veered in and out of mental stability.

And yet, the sixteenth president of the United States won a civil war, vanquished the institution of slavery, signed legislation to establish engineering and agricultural colleges and the homesteading of the West, and succinctly summarized the American ideal in a brief address at Gettysburg. There was a lot more behind the beard than a disagreeable face, making Lincoln arguably one of America's greatest presidents.

A COMMON PURPOSE

In a democracy, individuals and parties often vie for political advantage, but during times of national crisis, such as the Civil War, such disputes appear unseemly at best and traitorous at worst. This dynamic was evident when Lincoln challenged New York Democratic Governor Horatio Seymour's loyalty for questioning the president's war program, especially the Emancipation Proclamation.

In a firm letter, Lincoln reminded Seymour that "the co-operation of your State, as that of others, is needed—in fact, is indispensable."[1] He further emphasized that the nation's very existence depended on eliminating the "difference of purpose between you and me."[2] Lincoln was firm; the war's success depended on preserving a single-minded purpose.

Just as Lincoln recognized that dissension, left unchecked, could ultimately undermine the war effort, educators need to realize that unchecked enmity, among either the faculty or within the classroom, will eventually undercut the positive culture necessary to achieve academic success.

Creating proper avenues to resolve disagreements and address criticisms is a necessary starting point for eliminating such detrimental conflicts. Nevertheless, there is a time to follow Lincoln's approach and directly confront inappropriate and divisive comments and actions. After all, educators do have one overriding common purpose—student success.

Question: What are some possible approaches for resolving conflict between educators and between students?

DISCERNING COUNSEL

Daily, Abraham Lincoln faced choices that were critical to the nation and to his own political fortunes. Whether appointing a bureaucrat to distribute cotton in captured Vicksburg or determining the fate of a man charged with "furnishing aid to the enemy," Lincoln often found himself dependent on the counsel of others for resolving these difficult issues.[3]

In the civil servant's case, Lincoln's advisors recommended his appointment as "a man of strict integrity and honor,"[4] while counsel advised no "mitigation [easing] of the sentence"[5] for the collaborator. Individually, the decisions were of little consequence; collectively, the decisions shaped a presidency.

The ability to accurately weigh the reliability of advice is a necessary skill for every leader, one that Lincoln developed through daily practice. Teachers and administrators also must make daily decisions that affect the fortunes of their students and their staff. One way an educator can judge the quality of advice is by the number of options the advice-giver provides.

If the advisor provides several options, it shows he or she is taking the time to look at multiple sides, is not making a hasty decision, and is not simply promoting a personal agenda. The individual receiving the advice should keep a record of each person's counsel to determine if the advice-giver has a record of accuracy. Educators should remember that seeking advice before making decisions is always wise; taking the time to thoroughly evaluate the advice is even wiser.

Question: How do you discern the quality of advice?

FOUNDATION FOR GENIUS

The Gettysburg Address is revered by the American people as the ideal summation of the American creed. The story behind this great document is that

Lincoln hurriedly jotted down a few ideas and was almost extemporaneous in the preparation and the presentation of his speech.

However, reality suggests the foundation for his genius was not a sudden burst of inspiration but, rather, an extensive acquaintance with the words and the ideas of a variety of great authors and orators including Daniel Webster, Supreme Court Justice John Marshall, and the Reverend Theodore Parker.

All three emphasized the role of the people in government, a theme Lincoln eloquently captured in his famous address when he affirmed "that this government of the people, by the people, for the people, shall not perish from the earth."[6] It took a Lincoln to masterfully summarize and communicate a theme that had been held and cherished by many great men before him.

Lincoln's Gettysburg Address was built on a foundation of prior knowledge; likewise, teachers should help students acquire a base of knowledge that will equip them to construct their own opinions and ideas. This approach includes exposing students to the great ideas of the past, teaching critical thinking skills to interpret and categorize the information they acquire, and helping students to develop a moral framework for each idea and expression they generate.

It is no less foolish to build a house without a foundation than for a student to build an opinion without the resource of prior knowledge. The goal is to develop independent thinkers who are not independent from the great ideas and truths of history. Lincoln's genius came out of such ideas and truths; students would do well to imitate him.

Question: What do you consider to be essential ideas, skills, or morals for equipping students with a successful foundation?

GETTYSBURG MOMENTS

Most historians agree that the battle of Gettysburg was the turning point of the Civil War. However, as President Lincoln's urgent message following the battle implied, a far greater prize beckoned: "If General Meade can complete his . . . destruction of Lee's army, the rebellion will be over."

Unfortunately for Lincoln, Meade failed to act, allowing Lee's weakened forces to escape across the Potomac River and continue the war. A clearly anguished president reprimanded his inept general writing, "The war will be prolonged indefinitely. . . .Your golden opportunity is gone, and I am distressed immeasureably [sic] because of it."[7]

Meade's inaction meant continued casualties and the introduction of total warfare in the South, a tactic that left a path of destruction and years of lingering bitterness and recrimination among Southern people.

Lincoln understood that there were critical moments to act and that vacillation would lead to immediate and far-ranging problems for the future. Similarly, the teacher or administrator who neglects to act promptly when confronted with a classroom disruption, or to contact a parent when a child demonstrates social or academic trouble, may find him or herself with a larger and more enduring problem in the future.

Every day presents educators with a "Gettysburg moment." When such moments arise, take advantage of the "golden opportunity" and act. Better to move forward today while the cost is small, then to wait and have someone become "distressed immeasurably."

Question: What is your most memorable "Gettysburg moment" and how did you resolve it?

"HATCHING THE EGG"

At last, the brutal years of the Civil War had concluded, and to mark the joyous occasion a banner hung near the Capitol proclaiming, "This is the Lord's doing, it is marvelous in our eyes." Such hopeful declarations aside, the bloody scars of war made rebuilding the nation and reinstating the southern states difficult.

This was especially true because of the North's insistence that defeated states like Louisiana had to abolish slavery, grant civil rights to former slaves, and provide freedmen with voting rights before they could be readmitted to the Union. Such obstacles to rebuilding the nation frustrated Lincoln.

Always a Union man first, he maintained the southern states had suffered enough and that their defects could be corrected after their reinstatement to the Union. In a slightly more agrarian tone he insisted, "We shall sooner have the fowl by hatching the egg than by smashing it."[8]

The essential question following the Civil War was how to properly restore the southern states—quickly or with added requirements as proof they had truly changed. The same basic question occurs in the school setting when a student is expelled for disciplinary reasons.

The critical issue is how quickly a teacher or administrator should reinstate such a student and if it should come with added stipulations as proof the student has reformed. Some educators lean toward Lincoln's "hatching the egg" approach that insists the suspended student has already been punished enough and should not be crushed with added expectation before returning.

Still, other educators believe a returning student should be required to take added steps to prove he or she deserves to return to school. Ultimately, while a student's previous behavior may justify proof of reform before readmittance, such requirements should be balanced with a genuine desire to see the student quickly reintegrated back into the school community.

Question: What do you believe is the best approach for reinstating an expelled student?

MARCHING WITH STUDENTS

Many parents experience the struggle of not having a child progress academically or socially as envisioned. The Lincolns could relate to this disappointment, as their fourth child, Tad, due to learning disabilities and a cleft palate, frustrated even his personal tutor with his absence of developmental growth.

But where the tutor failed, Lincoln's military guard found a way to connect with the young boy. Upon their invitation, Tad became a regular visitor to the guards and soon became a favorite of the troops, marching side by side with them while dressed in his own miniature replica uniform. Such was their affection for Tad, the presidential guard even made him an honorary lieutenant.[9] Thanks to the soldier's actions, Tad found acceptance and purpose.

In every school, and most likely in every classroom, teachers will find "Tads" struggling with learning challenges. Undoubtedly, for every struggling student, there is an equally frustrated educator battling to help the student succeed. Fortunately, the guard's actions are an instructive tool to address the problem.

By allowing Tad to march with them and by assigning him a rank, the sentries acknowledged Tad's fundamental value. Educators should do no less. To help the Tad in your classroom gain confidence and excel academically, the teacher should identify and highlight the pupil's other qualities such as effort, perseverance, and creativity.

It is equally important to let the student know he or she is not alone in his or her struggles but is part of a troop moving forward together toward success. Do not wait another day to act; it is time to get marching with your out-of-step students.

Question: How do you build confidence in students struggling with learning disabilities?

PREVAILING SPIRIT

Lincoln, continually perplexed and disappointed by his generals during the Civil War, reluctantly named Major General Hooker as the new commander of the Union forces in the East. In a letter to Hooker, Lincoln detailed the cause of his apprehension:

"I much fear that the spirit which you have aided to infuse in the army, of criticizing their commander [General Burnside] and withholding confidence from him, will now turn upon you." Criticism's ill effect on the Union Army was distressingly clear to President Lincoln.

He concluded that not even Napoleon "could get any good out of an army while such a spirit prevails in it."[10] Hooker's critical spirit had permeated the army, and now, ironically, he stood as the likely recipient of its mischief.

If Lincoln were referring to a school rather than an army, he might restate his concern over unmerited criticism by saying, "Not even a great administrator could get any good out of a school faculty while such a spirit prevails in it." When criticism becomes the prevailing spirit within a faculty, its lingering effects can be devastating to staff morale and to successful teaching in the classroom.

To build a healthy work environment, educators must learn to distinguish between constructive criticism, designed to help a colleague address a professional or personal blind spot, and destructive criticism, which, like General Hooker, seeks advantage by undermining an associate. Avoiding criticism is not enough; educators must also intentionally cultivate and "infuse" a positive spirit into the workplace.

Creating a positive spirit starts by thanking the teacher who stays late to grade or supervise, by encouraging and coaching the colleague struggling with discipline or lesson planning, and by taking time to acknowledge each coworker's strengths. Just as one general can destroy an army, one encouraging teacher can start rebuilding a school.

Question: How can you personally help infuse a positive prevailing spirit at your school?

SOMETHING LARGER THAN SELF

The historian Joshua Shenk believed Lincoln's presidency was governed by "transcendent wisdom." Such leaders "guided by a sense of something larger than themselves will look past the petty concerns of the self." This worldview enabled Lincoln to overlook many vindictive insults and criticisms, maintaining his energy for more important ends.

Whether in person or through his letters, Lincoln demonstrated a "patience and grace" that consistently championed the restoration of his adversaries over political and personal victory.[11] He intuitively knew that a bitter man would be incapable of both winning the war and restoring the Union.

Like Lincoln, educators often experience sharp blows of criticism and dissent from parents, students, and even peers. Sometimes it is necessary to confront and find healing closure to such criticisms. However, teachers wishing to copy Lincoln's practice of transcendent wisdom must make a habit of looking past such slights by focusing on the greater goal of helping students succeed.

Such educators must take an even more difficult step: they must overcome hurt feelings and work to restore the critical parent, student, or peer to a place of partnership so that together they can work on behalf of the adolescents who need assistance. With the great number of youths in need of academic and social help, there is little room for selfish interest or resentment to limit teacher effectiveness. For the sake of students, transcend the small.

Question: What ideal, related to teaching, is larger than you and your personal interests?

THE MUSIC TONIC

Lincoln loved music. It provided the often careworn president an outlet for relaxation and reflection and offered a "tonic" for the gloominess that sometimes permeated his life. Lincoln's introspective personality found solace in moving and emotional musical pieces that matched his mood during the long and painful war years.

Interestingly, as a young lawyer, Lincoln was not above the revelry of singing with his peers; however, as his responsibilities increased, his carefree public singing diminished.[12] Eventually, he replaced participatory singing with theater and concert attendance, where he could experience anonymity and rest from the pressing realities of family crises, military burdens, and political intrigues.

The window into the impact of music on President Lincoln is also a window into what impacts student learning in the classroom today. Lincoln presented a valuable illustration of several types of intelligences students incorporate during the learning process, including music intelligence (thinking in a musical context), intrapersonal intelligence (personal feelings), and interpersonal intelligence (social interaction).

Lincoln's intrapersonal musical nature found refuge and space for contemplation through immersion in music, while his interpersonal musical temperament found a source of commonality with his friends and coworkers in sing-alongs. Today, music provides a similar opportunity for students to reflect, to regroup, and to connect with peers. Music may be just the approach needed to engage the Lincoln in your classroom.

Question: How are you meeting the needs of the interpersonal and intrapersonal student through music?

WHAT IS SUCCESS WORTH

1864 was a critical year in the Civil War, and not exclusively because of the battles on the field. A political contest for president was unfolding between Abraham Lincoln and General George McClellan. The outcome of the election was crucial to America's future: McClellan promised to end the war if he won; Lincoln promised to fight the war to its finish.

President Lincoln had several electoral advantages in the contest. For instance, as the commander-in-chief, he increased the mostly pro-Lincoln soldiers' vote by allowing disabled soldiers immediate leave to return home and vote. He also allowed soldiers already on leave additional time to vote.

Nevertheless, Lincoln unmistakably put the good of the Union ahead of his own political success, refusing to cancel the unpopular draft and declining to bring troops home from the front to vote. As Lincoln noted, "What is the Presidency worth to me if I have no country?"[13]

President Lincoln felt great pressure to win reelection in 1864; likewise, teachers often feel the weight of preparing students for standardized testing and of meeting parental expectations that their children receive only A's or B's. To meet these demands, teachers often teach to the test, sometimes losing sight of the chief objective of education—the training of productive and ethical citizens.

Achieving high scores or grades is insufficient if it means ignoring other important goals such as the development of character, critical thinking, creativity, and an inquisitive mind. Lincoln realized winning the presidency was meaningless if he lost the war. Ultimately, a score or grade is meaningless if a student leaves school transformed neither as a person nor as a learner.

Question: What do you believe a successful graduate looks like?

DEBRIEFING EXERCISE

Music was very important for President Lincoln's mental well-being. Identify the five songs that help your mental well-being as an educator. Explain why and then share them with a colleague.

1. When I am overwhelmed, I listen to. . .
   Why?
2. When I need motivation, I listen to. . .
   Why?
3. When I am frustrated, I listen to. . .
   Why?

4. When I need inspiration, I listen to. . .
   Why?
5. When I fail, I listen to. . .
   Why?

NOTES

1. The Lincoln Log: A Daily Chronology of the Life of Abraham Lincoln, Abraham Lincoln to Horatio Seymour, 23 March 1863, *CW*, 6:145-46; Alexander J. Wall, *A Sketch of the Life of Horatio Seymour 1810-1886* (Lancaster, PA: Lancaster Press, 1929), 23-25, http://www.thelincolnlog.org/view/1863/3/23

2. *Collected Works of Abraham Lincoln,* Volume 6, *Lincoln, Abraham, 1809-1865,* http://quod.lib.umich.edu/cgi/t/text/textidx?c=lincoln;rgn=div1;view=text;idno=lincoln6;node= lincoln6%3A314

3. *Collected Works of Abraham Lincoln,* Volume 8, *Lincoln, Abraham, 1809-1865,* To Joseph Holt, Judge Advocate General, September 16, 1864, A. Lincoln., http://quod.lib.umich.edu/l/lincoln/lincoln8/1:17

4. *Collected Works of Abraham Lincoln,* Volume 8, *Lincoln, Abraham, 1809-1865.* To William P. Fessenden, September 16, 1864, Annotation: [1] Parke-Bernet Catalog 905, December 1-2, 1947, No. 278, http://quod.lib.umich.edu/l/lincoln/lincoln8/1:19.

5. Collected Works of Abraham Lincoln, Volume 8, *Lincoln, Abraham, 1809-1865.* To Joseph Holt, Judge Advocate General, September 16, 1864, A. Lincoln. http://quod.lib.umich.edu/l/lincoln/lincoln8/1:17

6. *Gettysburg Address Abraham Lincoln Civil War Speech*, Genesis of the Gettysburg Address, retrieved 8/23/12. http://americancivilwar.com/north/lincoln.html#undergod

7. Lincoln Message Discovered at the National Archives, Abraham Lincoln to General-in-Chief Henry Halleck. Records of the Adjutant General's Office, National Archives, ARC identifier: 1257664. http://www.archives.gov/press/press-releases/2007/nr07-108.html. National Archives/Press/Journalist/Press Releases/Year June 7, 2007/

8. Epstein, Daniel Mark. *The Lincolns: Portrait of a Marriage*, New York: Ballantine Books, 2008, pages 496-497.

9. Pinsker, Mathew, "The Soldiers' Home," in *Abraham Lincoln: Great American Historians on Our Sixteenth President,* Brian Lamb and Susan Swain, eds., New York: PublicAffairs, 2008, pages 151-153.

10. Library of Congress: The Alfred Whital Stern Collection of Lincolniana [Letter to Joseph Hooker from Lincoln, January 26, 1863], retrieved 11/6/2012. http://memory.loc.gov

11. Shenk, Joshua Wolf. *Lincoln's Melancholy: How Depression Challenged a President and Fueled His Greatness*, Boston: Houghton Mifflin Company, 2005, page 202-203.

12. Featured Book: Kenneth A Bernard, *Lincoln and the Music of the Civil War*, pages 1-9, retrieved 9/17/2012. http://www.abrahamlincolnsclassroom.org/Library/newsletter.asp?ID=29&CRLI=109&searchWord=Lincoln%20%And%20%The%20%Music%20%Of%20%The%20%Civil%20%War.

13. Sandburg, Carl. *Abraham Lincoln: The Prairie Years and the War Years,* One-Volume Edition, San Diego: A Harvest Book—Harcourt, Inc., 1982, pages 558-559.

Chapter 5

Theodore Roosevelt

"I am entitled to the medal, and I want it."
—Theodore Roosevelt

He was boisterous, energetic, and irrepressible. He came from upstate New York wealth, but willingly plunged into the socially inferior profession of state politics, became a cowboy and lawman, led the charge up San Juan Hill (making him the undisputed hero of the Spanish-American War), became the police commissioner of New York City, vice president for President McKinley, and then the twenty-sixth president of the United States.

A Nobel Peace Prize, the creation of countless national parks, monuments, and national forests, innovative trust-busting, and a Panama Canal, earned him the distinction of having his likeness chiseled on Mount Rushmore. All of this came from a man who had debilitating childhood asthma, was bullied as a youth, and overcame the death of his beloved wife to kidney disease. In the end, Teddy Roosevelt had to charge up more than one hill in life to become a hero and a great leader.

AN EFFECTIVE COROLLARY

Like a small child standing up to the playground bully, America stood up to the European powers of the early nineteenth century by establishing the Monroe Doctrine. The doctrine plainly, if somewhat naively, demanded that Europeans stop meddling in the affairs of the Western Hemisphere.

Approximately eighty years later, an industrialized and newly empowered America, led by the indomitable Teddy Roosevelt, fortified the Monroe Doctrine with the Roosevelt Corollary. This new policy claimed authority for America to exercise "international police power" in the Americas.

A strong America could now truly enforce this policy.[1] Essentially, the president added the Roosevelt Corollary to check European ambitions, while skillfully using the existing Monroe Doctrine as justification for his new policy.

Roosevelt's ability to link a new practice with an already established policy also works when implementing a new idea or program at school. Although change is an inevitable part of the educational process, so is the resistance it generates by teachers, parents, administrators, and students.

To mitigate such opposition, a wise leader should follow Roosevelt's example and attach the new procedure or idea to an already accepted practice or concept. This ensures that the new policy flows out of a framework of familiarity and stability, which will arouse less dissension. For example, if changing curriculum at school, first identify the essential curricular concepts to maintain and build upon, and then amend these core principles with the newer standards or course additions. Innovation works best and is less unsettling when the unknown is linked to the known.

Question: How would you link a needed change to a current school practice?

BALANCING ON A FENCE

The presidential election of 1912 experienced a legendary political split between conservative Republican Howard Taft and progressive Republican Theodore Roosevelt, ultimately leading to the election of Democrat Woodrow Wilson. The Republican rift caused Secretary of War Henry Stimson, a member of Taft's cabinet, a great deal of anxiety, forcing him to choose between his friendship with Roosevelt and his loyalty to Taft.

The secretary desired not to alienate either candidate, but reluctantly chose loyalty to Taft. "I have thought all along that Mr. Taft should be renominated . . . I am a poor hand at keeping quiet and balancing on a fence." To soften the blow to Roosevelt, he added, "It is hard to look forward to a time when I am not working or thinking with you."[2]

At first, Roosevelt's response was amiable to Stimson's decision, but the heat of the campaign revealed a vindictiveness that led to a three-year schism in their friendship. World War I reunited the former colleagues, and the friendship remained until Roosevelt's death in 1919.

Stimson's noble attempt "of balancing on a fence" between presidential candidates, while failing in the short term, was nuanced enough to permit Roosevelt to renew his friendship and alliance with Stimson at a later time. Educators seeking to remain neutral in conflicts between coworkers are wise to imitate Stimson's thoughtful approach.

Sometimes picking sides is necessary, but it should be done in a way that protects everyone's dignity and innate desire to be accepted. If a side must be chosen, it is essential that the choice not be perceived as personal, and an avenue to work together on mutual points of interest in the future remains open.

Roosevelt and Taft split a party and lost an election; similarly, intemperate educators, unable to amicably resolve their differences, may divide a school. Every faculty needs a Stimson-like person to step forward and deescalate the problem.

Question: How do you maintain equitable and friendly relationships with coworkers during a disagreement?

CREATING A SAFE ENVIRONMENT

In 1904, the Japanese and Russians began a tenacious war for empire, with China serving as the main theater of imperialist ambition. It soon became evident on the field of battle that the smaller Japanese army was more than a match for the larger Russian military.

A worried Theodore Roosevelt, who originally applauded the Japanese upstart, now looked to resolve the conflict before Japan ruled Asia and excluded American trade and influence from the region. To avoid such an outcome, Roosevelt invited representatives of the Russian government and the Japanese government to confer on his yacht in Oyster Bay, a beautiful cove near his home in upstate New York.

The negotiations would not be easy. The president faced multiple diplomatic challenges, as the two parties fought over trivialities such as who would enter the room first, who would sit on Roosevelt's right, and which national cuisine would be the main course; additionally, he had to address the Japanese cultural sensitivity to the height discrepancy between each country's diplomats.[3] The president brilliantly addressed each concern*[4] winning the Nobel Peace Prize for resolving the Russo-Japanese War.

Theodore Roosevelt successfully negotiated a treaty between Japan and Russia because he created a safe environment for dialogue and for the exchange of ideas and solutions. Likewise, a successful teacher anticipates possible distractions and obstacles to effective learning by being attuned to the class dynamic, by strategically designing seating charts, by creating cooperative learning groups that mitigate unnecessary conflicts, and by identifying student insecurities that might limit participation and positive classroom interaction.

It takes planning and effective management, like Roosevelt's, to reduce learning distractions and to create an environment where students feel safe to learn.

Question: What steps can you take in anticipation of possible conflicts and distractions to limit their negative impact on learning?

*Problems and Solutions:

1. Who would enter the room first—*Roosevelt grasped both diplomats' arms and escorted them into the room simultaneously.*
2. Who would sit on Roosevelt's right during negotiations—*Roosevelt seated the diplomats strategically next to each other while he stood and moved around the room, even eating his dinner upright.*
3. Which nation's cuisine would be the main course—*He served uniquely American dishes honoring different regions of the United States.*
4. The height discrepancy between diplomats—*Almost all of the negotiations occurred while seated.*

ENERGY, FIDELITY, AND INTELLIGENCE

Teddy Roosevelt, while a strong proponent of capitalism, believed government played a central role in limiting its excesses. One such excess Roosevelt wanted to curtail was the monopoly. He believed that when one business came to dominate an industry, it ultimately prevented other businesses from reaching their full potential.

"Our aim," wrote Roosevelt, "is so far as possible to provide such conditions that there shall be equality of opportunity where there is equality of energy, fidelity, and intelligence; when there is a reasonable equality of opportunity the distribution of rewards will take care of itself."[5] Hence, Roosevelt believed the government was to support "equality of opportunity" for all business, not equality of outcomes. For this, each business had to succeed on its own merits. President Roosevelt's formula for facilitating business success is a practical model for producing achievement in the classroom. Creating "equality of opportunity" for all students is essential.

Educators should prevent monopolies that limit student "energy, fidelity, and intelligence" by curbing individual students from dominating classroom discussions, by providing multiple avenues for student feedback, and by incorporating a range of learning styles to address the unique needs of each student. In the end, when no one student, or type of student, has a monopoly on the teacher's time or attention, then every child has a chance to succeed on his or her own merits.

Question: What steps can you take to limit certain students from monopolizing your classroom?

GRADE OF HONOR

During the Spanish-American War, Theodore Roosevelt was one of the more colorful and heroic figures of the conflict, gaining distinction for leading the famed Rough Riders in the capture of the strategically vital San Juan Hill. At war's end, the ever ambitious Roosevelt lobbied the military to award him the Medal of Honor, "I am entitled to the medal, and I want it."

However, even with testimony from fellow officers that he "was among the very first to reach the crest of the hill," that "his life was placed in extreme jeopardy," and that his "fearlessness inspired his men," Roosevelt was denied the coveted medal.[6] Simply stated, the military felt that Roosevelt, though brave, merely did what was expected of all officers—lead men into battle. Later, Roosevelt concurred "that the board which declined to award it [the Medal of Honor] took exactly the right position."[7]

Many students have a touch of Theodore Roosevelt in them, lobbying for better grades or recognition for their accomplishments. The teacher, like the military board that awards medals, must establish clear guidelines or a rubric to determine proper grades or credit.

Clear expectations limit the subjective influence of unduly persuasive students or parents from the process. Students and teachers should also have a shared idea of which actions rise above basic requirements and demonstrate exceptional distinction worthy of reward. Succinctly, grades and recognition should rest on merit alone.

Question: How do you ensure that grades, extra credit, or verbal praise are awarded fairly?

IDENTIFYING THE ESSENTIALS

Having lost the election of 1912, Teddy Roosevelt looked forward to the distraction of a new adventure. Joining an expedition to survey and map the River of Doubt, an unexplored waterway that moved mysteriously through the rain forest of Brazil, offered the perfect opportunity. However, the journey quickly turned from a mere diversion for the former president into a potentially deadly affair.

Excessively concerned about the comfort of the journey's dignitaries, the team packed numerous frivolous incidentals, prematurely exhausting the pack animals. At Roosevelt's request, and to save the expedition, each man was required to eliminate all but "sheer necessities."[8] Even the scientists gathering specimens for the American Museum of Natural History were forced to discard valuable samples they collected.

Kermit, Roosevelt's son and companion on the trip, parted with many items but refused to discard his books, which he deemed indispensable to his well-being.[9] The younger Roosevelt recognized the difference between necessities and luxuries.

Theodore Roosevelt's foresight, encouraging his fellow travelers to discard unnecessary items, probably saved the expedition and enabled them to explore the entire River of Doubt. Educators also have goals or destinations they wish their students to reach. An ability to distinguish between essential material and nonessential material is critical for a teacher to identify like it was for Roosevelt's party of adventurers.

Lessons burdened with unnecessary information, such as off-point details and activities, can distract from the central ideas a teacher wants his or her students to learn and retain. Sometimes, even important concepts must be discarded if the main objective is to be achieved. Conquering educational "rivers of doubt" requires teachers who can discern between frivolous lesson incidentals and the "sheer necessities" essential for success.

Question: How do you distinguish between essential teaching material and nonessential teaching material?

SAVE BY EFFORT

In 1899, the future vice president Teddy Roosevelt gave a widely heralded speech in Chicago challenging Americans to embrace "the strenuous life, the life of toil and effort, of labor and strife."[10] Later, Roosevelt identified the key to national and individual success proclaiming, "In this life we get nothing save by effort."[11]

For the future president, there was no alternative to hard work and struggle for achieving success. He feared the coming generation would lose the essential frontier spirit of its ancestors which had made America a great nation.[12] Consequently, as president, Roosevelt modeled hard work and effort, and even strife, fostering an administration known for its energy and active approach to government.

Roosevelt's insistence that effort is critical to success is a wonderful reminder that classical instructional practices such as scaffolding, drill and practice, and collaborative learning are insufficient on their own.

To illustrate the link between effort and success, highlight hardworking and successful historical figures. Persuasive examples include George Washington Carver, an experimentally persistent African American scientist; Elizabeth Blackwell, a determined groundbreaking female doctor; and, yes, Teddy Roosevelt, a dynamic and tireless president.

Inspire students to choose the difficult, to embrace the frontier spirit that is not afraid of the unknown, and to prefer the path that requires hard work to achieve success. Help each young scholar realize what effort can accomplish in his or her life.

Question: Can you describe how the effort of one of your students helped him or her succeed?

SIX THOUSAND OBJECTS OF INTEREST

Two years removed from his presidency, Theodore Roosevelt was enjoying a memorable hunting trip in Africa, one of the largest expeditions of its kind in modern history. His hunting prowess, already legendary, was proving merited. The beneficiary of his conquests was the newly initiated Smithsonian Institute which commissioned the former president to collect zoological artifacts for its new museum.

His success was staggering, collecting over "6,000 objects of interest, including the skins and hides of animals . . . hundreds of rare birds, reptiles, fishes, botanical specimens, native implements, utensils and other ethnological [study of ethnic groups] material of great scientific value and intense human interest."[13] Because of Roosevelt's efforts, and the corresponding Smithsonian exhibition, thousands of citizens were exposed to the wonders of Africa, sparking their imaginations and equipping their understanding of the previously labeled Dark Continent.

Theodore Roosevelt understood that the average American would never see Africa and its rich and varied people, wildlife, and fauna. Consequently, the former president made it his personal ambition to bring the African experience to Americans.

Similarly, the typical student will never encounter many scientific, cultural, historical, artistic, or musical experiences unless there is a teacher willing to go and find eyewitnesses, specimens, artifacts, or stories to serve as visual and tangible examples of each. While teachers probably will never match Roosevelt's six thousand objects of interest, providing at least one experiential sample for each lesson may make all the difference between a student knowing about a subject and a student experiencing a subject.

Question: What is an object of interest you use in your class to spark student interest and imagination?

STRENGTHENING THE HANDS

Rejected as the standard bearer for the Republican Party during the election of 1912, Teddy Roosevelt quickly became the nominee for the Progressive Party. His acceptance speech at the Progressive National Convention, delivered with characteristic exuberance, embraced several causes that were provocative and forward-thinking for their time, none more so than his call for women's suffrage.

Roosevelt argued directly that, "if women could vote they would strengthen the hands of those who are endeavoring to deal in efficient fashion with evils."[14] He envisioned women, currently stymied in their efforts to address the ills of society, using the power of the vote to relieve the suffering they witnessed daily in society.

Roosevelt believed it was essential to vest all citizens, including women, with the right to vote, knowing full well it was the chief pathway to relevance in a democracy. Similarly, a successful educator can empower or "strengthen the hands" of each student by requesting their input in the educational process—both what to learn and how to learn it.

Empowered students are no longer mere observers of learning, they are facilitators and difference makers. They have a vested interest to see their ideas and decisions be realized and implemented. Such empowerment can include students choosing from a teacher-provided list of books to read, selecting a debate topic, or picking a specific learning approach to study a subject. Give your students a vote in the learning process and see how it can strengthen their hands to learn.

Question: How do you strengthen the hands of your students so that they are part of the learning process?

THE BUCHANAN PRINCIPLE

In the early years of the Roosevelt Administration, a life or death drama unfolded as an increasingly bitter coal miner's strike erupted. New York Mayor Seth Low predicted that without coal to heat people's homes "MILLIONS OF INNOCENT PEOPLE . . . WILL ENDURE REAL SUFFERING IF THE PRESENT CONDITIONS CONTINUE."[15]

As such dire warnings reached President Roosevelt, he quickly assembled his advisors to address the growing crisis. All but Attorney General Philander Knox believed strikers and management should meet quickly to resolve the dispute.

The president agreed with the majority and ignored Knox, believing he suffered from "the Buchanan principle* of striving to find some constitutional reason for inaction."[16] The administration's energetic response brought the contentious strike to a successful conclusion and made Roosevelt the first president to ever arbitrate a work stoppage between management and labor.

Caution, whether exhibited by members of a president's cabinet or by educators in an academic setting, can be a valuable quality. However, too much caution can undermine needed educational innovation and adaptation. A good leader must discern between genuine advice that recommends restraint and the advice of individuals who perpetually advocate "the Buchanan principle of striving to find some . . . reason for inaction."

Consider a few simple questions when determining the value of people's advice: (1) Do they have a vested interest in the outcome of the decision? (2) Do they have a history of excessive caution or disproportionate action? (3) Was their previous advice appropriate for the situation? Sometimes, a Buchanan-like advisor can keep you from taking imprudent risks, just make sure he or she does not keep you from making difficult and necessary changes.

James Buchanan was president prior to the Civil War. Many have argued, including Teddy Roosevelt, that Buchanan used the Constitution as an excuse for inaction as regional difference intensified, thus allowing the South to slide into secession and the nation into civil war.

Question: How do you distinguish between prudent advice and overly cautious advice?

DEBRIEFING EXERCISE

1. What are three areas of your life you practice the Buchanan Principle and make excuses for not acting?
2. What are concrete action steps you can take to overcome the inaction you listed above?
3. Provide a specific date to take action on each step listed above and a person to hold you accountable.

NOTES

1. Bailey, Thomas A. *A Diplomatic History of the American People*, Sixth Edition, New York: Appleton-Century-Crofts, Inc., 1958, 183-184 and 505.
2. Stimson, Henry L., and Bundy, McGeorge. *On Active Service in Peace and War*, New York: Harper & Brothers, 1948, pages 50–54.

3. Gerson, Noel B. *TR: A Biographical Novel about Theodore Roosevelt*, New York: Doubleday and Company, 1970, pages 298-303.

4. Ibid.

5. Evolution of the Conservation Movement, 1850-1920, Report of the National conservation commission. February, 1909. Special message from the President of the United States transmitting a report of the National conservation commission, with accompanying papers, Image 10 of 279, page 4. http://memory.loc.gov

6. Yockelson, Mitchell, "I Am Entitled to the Medal of Honor and I Want It": Theodore Roosevelt and His Quest for Glory, *Prologue Magazine*, Spring 1998, Vol. 30, No. 1. http://www.archives.gov/publications/prologue/1998/spring/roosevelt-and-medal-of-honor-1.html

7. Ibid.

8. Millard, Candice. *The River of Doubt: Theodore Roosevelt's Darkest Journey*, New York: Broadway Books, 2005, pages 112-113.

9. Ibid.

10. Theodore Roosevelt Association: Speeches, Research/Resources on TR, The Strenuous Life, retrieved 12/13/2012. http://www.theodoreroosevelt.org/research/speech%20strenuous.htm.

11. Theodore Roosevelt, "The Strenuous Life" (10 April 1899), Leroy G. Dorsey, Texas A&M University, last updated July 11, 2007, http://archive.vod.umd.edu/internat/tr1899int.htm, retrieved 12/18/2018.

12. Ibid.

13. Everett, Marshall, and others, *Roosevelt's Thrilling Experiences in the Wilds of Africa and Triumphal Tour of Europe*, A. Hamming, 1910, pages 46, 161-162.

14. Russell, Thomas H., A. M., LL. D. Editor-in-Chief. *The Political Battle of 1912: Party Platforms, National Issues, Great Leader:* Official Edition, L. h. Walter, 1912, page 108.

15. Morris, Edmund. *Theodore Rex*, New York: The Modern Library, 2001, pages 150-152.

16. Ibid.

Chapter 6

Herbert Hoover

"The government shall not compete with or replace any of them but shall add to their initiative and their strength."—Herbert Hoover

Hoover's name was intertwined with the Great Depression. For example, the mushroom-like shacks of the unemployed that sprang up on the edge of most American cities during the 1930s were called Hoovervilles, while newspapers used by the homeless to cover themselves and stay warm at night were euphemistically called Hoover blankets.

Eventually, the once popular president was linked to almost every negative aspect of the terrible economic collapse. However, Hoover was more than the caricature ascribed to him by his critics. He was an orphan, a Quaker, spoke fluent Chinese, studied geology at Stanford, became a millionaire in the mining industry, served as Secretary of Commerce for two presidents, and most amazingly, orchestrated the rescue of millions of starving Europeans following WWI.

Herbert Hoover's name and legacy deserves to be more than a multiple-choice question in which the Great Depression is the only correct answer.

"ADD TO THEIR INITIATIVE AND THEIR STRENGTH"

The Great Depression was destabilizing to the world. In desperation, many nations turned to authoritarian and centralizing ideologies, such as Communism and Fascism, hoping a strong central government would minimize the damage of the growing economic downturn. President Hoover moved to check the growth of such undemocratic forces in America.

Hoover did this by clearly defining the limits of the federal government's power over state and local governments and over individual citizens. He maintained that "the government shall not compete with or replace any of them but shall add to their initiative and their strength."[1] In other words, he asserted that the central government existed to aid smaller governments reach their full potential, not assume their responsibilities.

The Great Depression caused many nations to reject the form of limited government Hoover advocated and turn to authoritarianism as an answer instead. Similarly, when a student disappoints academically, parents and educators may want to increase their authority and control over the child. However, excessive adult intervention risks stunting a young person's ability to develop the coping skills necessary to respond to life's challenges.

Insisting that each student lives up to his or her full potential is a better approach. The secret is to not expect less of a struggling student, nor intervene in a manner that undermines a student's initiative, but rather, to add to the individual's strengths and enterprise by setting high expectations, by providing necessary resources, and by contributing practical and inspiring guidance. Successfully ending a student's academic depression requires increased student responsibility, not less.

Question: How do you determine the amount of help a parent or teacher should provide a student struggling with academics?

ARISETH A LITTLE CLOUD

The Great Depression shook America and the world. President Hoover recorded in his memoirs that he could see financial trouble coming several years before the economy crashed. Using this scriptural reference (see 1 Kings 18:44), the former president displayed his discernment writing,*[2] "A cloud as small as a man's hand is rising from the sea." So Elijah said, "Go and tell Ahab, 'Hitch up your chariot and go down before the rain stops you.'"[3]

However, unlike Elijah, Hoover spied not one but several little clouds that threatened a mighty storm of economic difficulty. These storm clouds included a growing stock-exchange bubble, where people paid more for stocks than they were worth; the challenge of moving from a war economy to a free market economy; and the increasingly irregular prices found in the commodities trade (buying merchandise).[4]

Sadly, for Hoover and the nation, he ignored these gathering clouds. He made overly optimistic assumptions that the economy would continue to grow and could withstand any new economic problems. Consequently, the storm came, and the chariots were unprepared for the Great Depression that followed.

Educators can learn from Hoover's missteps and false optimism. Confronting the little clouds of education (students turning in low-quality work, an unkind remark by one student toward another student, a disrespectful comment toward a teacher or principal, or any of a thousand other minor infractions) can prevent a great storm of problems later.

Therefore, if a student turns in low-quality work, insist they do better, provide them necessary help, and then identify the consequences if the student does not show an effort to improve.

Notice a student speaking unkindly to another student or being disrespectful to an adult? Pull him or her aside, discover the motive, and then take corrective action so that it does not happen again. Hoover saw little clouds and overlooked them; educators cannot afford to make the same mistake.

Question: What little cloud do you need to intercept before it becomes a storm of difficulties?

EASE OF SUCCESS

Is it possible that too much success early in one's life can limit success later in life? Yes, according to political scientist Richard Hofstadter. He believed Herbert Hoover's development as a leader was stunted, in part, because success in the mining business required too little effort and diminished his incentive "to learn deeply from anything outside of it."[5]

This lack of adversity left Hoover untested and caused the previously successful businessman and humanitarian to fail as president.[6] Hence, as the crisis known as the Great Depression unfolded, Hoover could not rally his government and the nation or compromise and work with people who might have helped him find a solution to the economic distress. A promising presidency was undermined. Easy success had produced hard failure.

Herbert Hoover's ease of success in business ironically made it more difficult for him to be an effective president. It is a cautionary tale for educators to not let students solely do coursework in areas they find success. An effective liberal arts education should require students to experience classes that challenge and help develop all aspects of their intelligences.

If a history, math, or English course is difficult for a student, do not allow him or her to drop the course immediately without first challenging the student to make every effort to succeed. Rather, encourage students to get tutors, come for extra-help classes, or increase their study time. Creating a culture where students are expected to step outside their natural area of comfort and develop a habit of fighting through difficulties is a recipe for future success.

Question: How do you challenge students to step outside their areas of comfort?

NO GREATER FRIEND

It is quite possible that twentieth-century Poland had no greater friend than Herbert Hoover. Following both World Wars, Poland found its people desperate and without food. Hoover became their champion, rallying America's will and resources* to feed thousands of starving Poles.

Although Hoover's humanitarian efforts were not limited to Poland, directing American aid to feeding millions of other hungry Europeans, his affinity and concern for Poland and her people was unique. Hoover did not merely fill Polish bellies, but fought for their liberty, too, criticizing the West's abandonment, for expediency, of Polish freedom to Russian occupation following WWII.[7]

The Hoover Institute aptly summed up the president's value to the Poles and to Europe writing, "For decades, Hoover was to the Poles and to millions of Europeans a symbol of faith, charity, and compassion, helping where there had been no hope and life seemed unbearable."[8]

Hoover's active lifelong concern for feeding and serving the people of Poland, even after much of the West abandoned the nation during the Cold War era, provides an excellent model for assisting academically and socially neglected students. First, Hoover saw a need, then he created a specific plan to meet the need, then he acted with the belief that everyone had value, and finally, he persevered through seemingly immovable obstacles to resolve the area of deficiency.

Today, there is a monument in Krakow, Poland, to commemorate Hoover's humanitarian efforts. For the educator who faithfully, and sometimes sacrificially, helps the struggling child, no one may build a monument, but to that child, the assisting teacher will always be the one who helped "where there had been no hope and life seemed unbearable." A teacher willing to act with "faith, charity, and compassion" can make all the difference in a child's life.

*Hoover helped fight hunger in Europe following WWI as head of the Food Administration. During the post–WWII era, he contributed by advising Harry S. Truman in the development of the Marshall Plan, a program that helped rebuild much of Europe.

Question: What is your plan of action to help an academically or socially challenged student?

NOT MY BABY

The worldwide depression of the early 1930s was placing an increasing strain on Europe's ability to pay off the debt and reparations incurred during World

War I.[9] Hoover, sensing that struggling European nations would collapse under the weight of their continuing payments, which would lead to a further weakening of the world's economy, negotiated a moratorium on war-related debt for a year.

However, a landslide loss to FDR put Hoover's plan in jeopardy. Acting immediately, the vanquished president urged the president-elect to extend his debt relief program. FDR, wanting to focus on economic issues at home, rather than on the unpopular European war debt issue, quipped the problem was "not my baby."[10] Shortly thereafter, six debtor nations defaulted, impacting the world's struggling economy even more. The problem was now Roosevelt's baby, too.

As FDR discovered, ignoring Hoover's advice for managing the international war debt crisis simply made the matter worse. Educators would be wise to avoid making a similar mistake when problems arise at their schools. Administrators, teachers, or parents who naively believe a struggling child, a disciplinary issue, or any other school-related problem is always someone else's concern risk creating far greater consequences in the future. It takes character to act in the face of outright opposition or willful indifference to such problems, especially when the solutions might be difficult or unpopular. Ultimately, most challenges cannot be ignored as someone else's "baby," they need people brave enough to take ownership and respond.

Question: What is one problem at school you can proactively commit to help resolve?

ON THE FEET OF HEALTHY CHILDREN

Leading a children's wellness convention during the early 1920s, Secretary of Commerce Herbert Hoover acknowledged "the sad deficiency in the protection of child health."[11] Assessing WWI draft records, Hoover lamented that of the 90 percent of children born healthy, by the time they reached military conscription age, only 30 percent were ruled fit for duty.

He believed too many young people were suffering from preventable diseases and health complications between childhood and adulthood. To improve the health of adolescents, the future president recommended better access to medical facilities, an enhanced immunization program, and increased communication with parents on childhood nutritional needs. Hoover desired to educate the nation on children's health issues, firmly believing that a "nation marches forward on the feet of healthy children."[12]

Hoover's awareness that children's health impacts a nation's well-being is a valuable reminder that today's students also face critical health issues. Maintaining proper nutrition, poor sleeping habits, and mental health challenges are all examples of modern concerns. Teachers are in a strategic position to daily observe students and report any health-related matters to the administration, the school nurse, and to the children's parents.

As Hoover observed, communication and education are critical for helping students and parents better understand and solve the wellness issues confronting today's students. Attentive and proactive teachers play an essential role in not only improving students' health today, but the nation's well-being tomorrow.

Question: What indicators do you look for to determine if a student's health is adversely impacting his or her academic success?

SEEDBEDS OF LEADERSHIP

President Hoover was convinced that small liberal arts colleges were "seedbeds of leadership."[13] He believed strongly that their educational model correctly emphasized "moral and spiritual qualities superior to mere material things, without which any purely economic system would collapse."[14]

Hoover maintained that leaders should never be trained for mere profit alone, but for imparting principles of "high character and noble ideals."[15] To achieve such worthy objectives, he underscored the importance of personal contact between the teacher and the pupil and the necessity of providing multiple "cultural opportunities for youth."[16]

The president's remarks on effective instruction are timeless markers of quality education, highlighting the value of relational instruction and the requisite exposure of young people to an assortment of ideas, art, history, and places. Successful educators inspire students to aim higher than simple material gain, envisioning them to pursue and become well-rounded people of character and excellence.

Such instructors are passionate not only about what they are teaching but about whom they are teaching. When the classroom is filled with principled reasoning, models of the possible, and a caring teacher, fertile ground is created where seedbeds of leadership can grow.

Question: How do you practice relational instruction, promote character-driven leaders, and create cultural opportunities for young people to grow?

THE TAXING TRIALS

By June 1931, President Hoover faced a growing federal deficit of over $200 million dollars. Even more startling, by the following fiscal year, government revenues had decreased 50 percent. Hoover diagnosed the problem and solution, bluntly stating that "national stability required that we balance the budget. To do this, we had to increase taxes on one hand and, on the other, to reduce drastically government expenditures."[17]

The president recognized the difficulty associated with capping government spending, as well as the political risks of raising taxes, especially in an election year. Nevertheless, given "the magnitude of the deficits . . . determined and courageous policies" became necessary to balance the budget.[18] Regardless of the wisdom of Hoover's plan, raising taxes was an unpopular and extradifficult lift for a fiscally conservative president.

Question: What issue(s) as a teacher or administrator do you sometimes find difficult to confront?

UNJUSTIFIED CRITICISM

A growing economic depression, and Hoover's reaction to it, was creating a perception of an ineffective and uncaring leader. Further eroding the president's standing was his response to unemployed WWI veterans descending on the nation's capital.

Made desperate by the economic crisis, the former soldiers camped out on the capitol grounds, demanding Hoover give them their military bonuses thirteen years early. At first, the president discreetly provided the Bonus Army, as they came to be called, with a partial advance on their bonus, as well as tents and food.

Ignoring Hoover's goodwill gesture, many veterans, holding out for their full bonuses, refused to leave. Hoover moved to have them peaceably removed from the capital grounds. Sadly, for Hoover's reputation, he chose the wrong officer for the task. A willfully disobedient Douglas MacArthur ignored the president's orders, resorting to violent force to remove the remaining veterans.

When criticism mounted across the nation over how the former soldiers were treated by the army, Hoover courageously took full responsibility for their ill-treatment, even though his orders for their peaceable removal had been expressly disobeyed.[19]

Education has its fair share of Bonus Armies, too, such as parents requesting a higher grade for their child, a more important part in the school play, or increased playing time on the sports team. If a teacher's actions unfairly cost a student a better grade or position, he or she should take responsibility and work to rectify the problem.

However, educators should not take the blame when it is unmerited. This may diminish respect for the teacher, as it did for Hoover, and make it harder to resolve problems in the future. Taking responsibility for poor educational decisions takes courage. Nevertheless, as President Hoover learned, accepting unjust criticism for the actions of others is harmful to a leader's future success.

Question: What is the proper balance between taking responsibility for a failure at school and protecting your credibility by exposing the real cause or person behind the problem?

UNNECESSARY FEARS AND APPREHENSION

Believing the country needed a different solution to address the rapidly escalating depression, Americans chose Franklin Roosevelt to replace Herbert Hoover as president. Seeking to reassure a fearful populous, Roosevelt famously declared that Americans had "nothing to fear but fear itself."[20]

Now forgotten, Hoover had similarly battled "unnecessary fears and apprehensions."[21] Such fear produced money hoarding, "idle business, idle men, and depreciated prices."[22] To break the deflationary cycle, Hoover encouraged Americans to return their money to the banks, convinced that such currency repatriation would stimulate the economy five to ten times more than in the hands of private individuals.

To assist in reaching this aim, he created the Reconstruction Finance Corporation to persuade citizens to patriotically stop hoarding money and return it to the banks to end the negative consequences of fear on the American economy.[23]

President Hoover quickly learned it was insufficient to merely encourage Americans to return their money to the banks. To produce positive results, and stop fear-driven currency hoarding, concrete actions such as President Roosevelt's Bank Holidays, which closed unstable banks until patrons were convinced their money was safe, were necessary.

Only then did Americans willingly return their money to their respective depositories. Similarly, educators cannot simply tell struggling pupils not to be afraid of math, science, or English; they must take concrete steps to help such students renew their effort to succeed. Suggesting a tutor, providing help classes, giving extra practice assignments, or specifying better study habits are all sound and practical starting points to help students overcome fear and achieve academic success.

Question: What practical assistance are you providing students to help them overcome their unnecessary fears and apprehension in your field of study?

DEBRIEFING EXERCISE

Directions: One of the challenges President Hoover faced was unjustified criticism. Interview five or six colleagues and ask them how they prefer to have criticism communicated to them. Then ask the same question of five or six students.

Based on your interviews...

1. What is the best way to deliver criticism to a peer?
2. What is the best way to deliver criticism to a student?
3. How do you prefer criticism be communicated to you? Why?
4. How will this exercise impact how you deliver criticism?

NOTES

1. Herbert Hoover Presidential Library and Museum: The Published Writings of Herbert Hoover, *The Memoirs of Herbert Hoover*, Volume 3: *The Great Depression 1929-1941*, New York: The Macmillan Company, 1952, page, http://www.ecommcode.com/hoover/ebooks/displayPage.cfm?BookID=B1&VolumeID=B1V3&PageID=1

2. *New International Version (NIV) Holy Bible, New International Version®, NIV® Copyright © 1973, 1978, 1984, 2011 by Biblica, Inc.® Used by permission. All rights reserved worldwide, https://biblehub.com/niv/1_kings/18.htm. *Note*: *I replaced the King James version used by Hoover with the NIV because it is easier for the modern reader to understand.*

3. Herbert Hoover Presidential Library and Museum, *Memoirs of Herbert Hoover*, Volume 3, pages 5 and 6.

4. Ibid.

5. Hofstadter, Richard. *The American Political Tradition: And the Men Who Made It*, New York: Alfred A. Knopf, 1968, page 289.

6. Ibid.

7. Siekierski, Maciej. History of a Friendship: Herbert Hoover and Poland; and Recalling the post-war relief efforts of the thirty-first president, SIDEBAR to Remembering the Warsaw Uprising, *Hoover Digest* » 2004 no. 4, retrieved 6/13/2013. http://www.hoover.org/publications/hoover-digest/article/7495, October 30, 2004.

8. Hoover Institution, Stanford University, An American Friendship: Herbert Hoover and Poland, June 1, 2005, to August 1, 2005, library and archives » exhibits, http://www.hoover.org/library-and-archives/exhibits/27245, retrieved 6/13/2013.

9. Most powers that participated in WWI had heavy war debts, with England and France owing money directly to the United States. However, the Treaty of Versailles, written by the victorious nations, required Germany alone to pay reparations for most of the damages resulting from the war.

10. Bailey, Thomas A. *A Diplomatic History of the American People*, Third Edition, New York: F. S. Crofts & Co., 1947, pages 721-723.

11. Herbert Hoover Presidential Library and Museum, *The Memoirs of Herbert Hoover*, Volume 2: *The Cabinet and the Presidency 1920-1933*, pages 97-98.

12. Ibid.

13. Herbert Hoover Presidential Library and Museum, *Public Papers of the Presidents of the United States: Herbert Hoover*, Volume 3: *1931*, page 409, Washington, DC, United States Government Printing Office, 1976, http://www.ecommcode.com/hoover/ebooks/displayPage.cfm?BookID=B2&VolumeID=B2V3&PageID=2

14. Ibid.

15. Ibid.

16. Ibid.

17. Herbert Hoover Presidential Library and Museum, *The Memoirs of Herbert Hoover*, Volume 3, pages 132, 133, and 136.

18. Ibid.

19. Miller Center, University of Virginia, U.S. Presidents, Herbert Hoover, see David Hamilton, Herbert Hoover: Domestic Affairs, section Hoover's New Approach, http://millercenter.org/president/hoover/domesticaffairs, retrieved 6/13/2013.

20. Herbert Hoover Presidential Library and Museum: The Published Writings of Herbert Hoover, *Public Papers of the Presidents of the United States: Herbert Hoover*, Volume 4: *1932-33*, page 41, http://www.ecommcode.com/hoover/ebooks/displayPage.cfm?BookID=B2&VolumeID=B2V4&PageID=84

21. Ibid.

22. Ibid.

23. Ibid.

Chapter 7

Franklin Roosevelt

"Act as a burr under the saddle and get things moving. . . . Step on it!"—
Franklin Roosevelt

He was a Roosevelt, connected, wealthy, handsome, and already on his way to making a name for himself, with the hope of one day matching his successful cousin Teddy Roosevelt. Indeed, his career path as a New York state politician, assistant secretary of the Navy, and a run at being vice president, gave all the marks of a bright political future.

Then adult polio struck. Overcoming paralysis, depression, and years of recovery to become the governor of New York and then an unheard-of four-term president—fighting an economic depression and a world war—is quite a testament to his perseverance and political skill. He was after all, a Roosevelt.

BENEFICIAL HUMOR

In the crossfire of the 1944 presidential election, congressional Republicans angrily accused FDR of wasting taxpayer money by frivolously sending a destroyer back to the Aleutian Islands to retrieve his forgotten dog, Fala.

The president quickly deflected the attacks with humor by musing, "Well of course, I don't resent attacks, and my family doesn't resent attacks, but Fala does resent them. You know, Fala is Scotch," and as such, her "Scotch soul was furious."[1] With this quip, the president muted the charges of financial lavishness, drolly implying that no frugal Scotty would ever stand for wasting taxpayer money.[2] Roosevelt's humor quickly calmed what might have become a glaring political liability to his reelection plans.

FDR understood the power of humor to connect with and in some instances disarm people. Likewise, humor is beneficial in academic settings, and when used appropriately, softens a disciplinary action, enlivens a dull class, deflates a tense moment, or even teaches an important principle.

However, it is recommended that educators use humor that is positive and constructive and not imitate the sometimes-sarcastic overtones employed by

Roosevelt. A famous proverb reminds people that "a cheerful heart is good medicine."[3] Fittingly, to have a healthy classroom, teachers should inject a little dose of humor into every lesson.

Question: How have you used humor to soften a disciplinary action, enliven a dull class, deflate a tense moment, or even teach an important principle?

CRITICS

Critics are an unavoidable part of life, and Franklin Roosevelt had his fair share. There were the more traditional detractors, like Republican politicians, who argued Roosevelt's New Deal programs were too aggressive and too dismissive of America's traditional capitalistic values. From the left came critics like radio personality Father Charles Coughlin and Louisiana Governor Huey P. Long.

They asserted that FDR did not go far enough in expanding government to end the suffering inflicted by the Great Depression. While Coughlin insisted Americans "not . . . become cannon fodder for the greedy system of an outworn capitalism nor factory fodder for the slave whip of communism," Long urged the American people to have "none too poor and none too rich," a goal he hoped to achieve by making the well-off "Share the wealth."[4]

More sensitive to the political threats from his left, Roosevelt sought to outmaneuver these critics by calling for a series of new taxes on the wealthy, designed to pay for programs to help the poor.[5] He believed his actions would refute his critics and demonstrate his concern for America's underprivileged.

Like Roosevelt, educators face criticism from multiple fronts, including parents, administrators, peers, and accrediting agencies. The essential question is how accommodating teachers should be toward such faultfinders. At a minimum, there ought to be a willingness to listen to and engage detractors, realizing they may have valuable insights and suggestions on how to improve as an educator.

Such professional humility, when paired with constructive changes, can have a positive effect on a teacher's development. On the other hand, teachers should recognize that critics are sometimes ill-informed and guided by improper motives such as insecurity, jealousy, or a mistaken interpretation of the situation.

On such occasions, a teacher must disregard the criticism and do what he or she deems right. In matters of criticism, teachers need both the humility to hear and change and the wisdom to be deaf to its unearned destructiveness.

Question: How do you determine when to accommodate a critic or challenge a critic?

FORESIGHT

FDR, in the midst of the Great Depression, was given great leeway by the people to fix the economy and turn the nation's economic fortunes around. The same latitude was not extended to preparing for war. An isolationist America, experiencing the sting of the depression and feeling safe behind the extensive moats of the Atlantic and the Pacific, was in no mood to enter yet another conflict in Europe or Asia.

Nevertheless, Roosevelt had the foresight to begin the difficult move toward war. Viewing Mussolini's incursions into Africa and the fascist-led civil war of Spain as warning signs of coming calamity, he pushed Congress to allocate money for the biggest peacetime military buildup in American history.[6] Roosevelt's discernment ultimately helped America prevail over the WWII fascist governments of Germany, Italy, and Japan.

FDR correctly predicted the coming war. Educators need similar discernment for understanding and anticipating educational trends, technological innovations, and societal influences, and how best to respond to each. Developing an appropriate response to such changes requires staying well-informed of current developments, regularly reading academic journals, and maintaining open channels of communications with peers across the nation.

Additionally, addressing the latest trends involves a willingness to adjust to new information as it becomes available. Ultimately, quality instruction requires FDR-like educators with the foresight to prevail over the enemies of academic success.

Question: What do you foresee as the necessary adjustments education will have to undergo to adapt to a changing world?

MAINTAINING TRUE OPTIMISM

In the waning days of WWII, the Big Three—Roosevelt, Churchill, and Stalin—convened at Yalta to determine the postwar fate of Europe. By many accounts, FDR fared poorly during the negotiations because of his increasingly debilitating circulatory health problems.

Others maintained the changing realities of the war undermined the United States's bargaining position, particularly the need for Russian assistance to defeat Japan. Consequently, to maintain the tenuous alliance between Russia and the United States, FDR allowed Poland to shift from German control to Russian domination.

Americans, unaware of these hidden complexities, became disillusioned when the president's optimistic promise of Polish independence did not materialize. Ultimately, the loss of Polish sovereignty to the Soviets created a perception that the Russians had reneged on the treaty and were untrustworthy allies. A Cold War between the two nations soon ensued.[7]

Educators often face collaboration problems like FDR's Yalta scenario. Such issues as budget cuts, hiring or firing, or disciplinary action can all lead to division in a school community. Misplaced optimism is no substitute for addressing stark differences between parties or for achieving real solutions.

While always wise to remain positive when negotiating through difficult issues, it is equally important to remain transparent and forthright with those who disagree on the best practice or solution to resolving the dispute. True optimism comes from finding real answers that are embraced by both sides in a disagreement. This takes hard work, humility, and candidness. Such actions can prevent a Cold War from developing in your school.

Question: What is the best way to maintain a positive atmosphere in a classroom or school and still be forthright about difficult issues?

MODEL COMMUNICATIONS

During the Great Depression anxiety and fear troubled millions of Americans. Into this cauldron of angst came the reassuring voice of President Roosevelt. Using the modern technology of the radio, FDR inspired and encouraged people to overcome their present difficulties with weekly pep talks that came to be known as Fireside Chats.

The positive response to these chats was not accidental. FDR had a well-scripted plan for communicating and connecting with his listening audience. He kept his talks "accessible and understandable" by keeping each one brief, by using basic vocabulary, and by using relatable anecdotes to connect with his listeners.[8] Additionally, FDR emphasized that the American people and he were in this fix together and that with a united effort they could overcome the economic and social challenges of their time.[9]

Roosevelt's idea of Fireside Chats, with their interest in keeping information "accessible and understandable," is an excellent model for teachers to imitate in the classroom. This practice stresses the importance of dividing information into smaller units, connecting the material to topics of interest, and incorporating age-appropriate language to help students maintain their focus on the content. It also emphasizes the advantage of shared responsibility when confronting difficult problems. Such an approach reassures students that while the teacher will not do their work, he or she will persist with them until they successfully learn the material.

Question: What steps can you take to make your lesson plans more "accessible and understandable" and to communicate a culture of shared responsibility with your students?

PENDERGAST-LIKE STUDENTS

The Kansas City of the 1930s was a wayward and rollicking town, run by the political boss Tom Pendergast. Not content to merely control a city, Boss Tom and his political machine ambitiously desired to control all of Missouri. Pendergast's power even touched the national scene, helping send Franklin Roosevelt to the White House in 1932.

Likewise, Truman's political career as a judge, and then as a United States Senator from Missouri, benefited from the machine's get-out-the-vote efforts. However, as the extent of Pendergast's corruption became public and his influence waned, Roosevelt chose to disassociate himself from the old boss.

But Truman, an intensely loyal man, maintained his support and friendship for the publicly sullied political boss. The decision was questionable, as Pendergast eventually went to jail for tax evasion, and his power and influence were eviscerated.[10]

Boss Tom had some clear deficiencies; even so, he played a key role in advancing the careers of two remarkable presidents. As in the case of Pendergast, educators must often deal with talented yet flawed students. Not unlike FDR and Truman, each teacher and administrator should determine to what extent he or she is willing to support such a pupil.

Administrators must also consider and balance a troubled student's impact on the classroom environment with the possibility that they will transition into a productive student and citizen. Ultimately, loyalty to a student is a principled action, but not if such support harms other students.

Question: What principles guide you when dealing with Pendergast-like students who have academic, athletic, musical, or social abilities, but also have clear and troubling deficiencies?

PREPARATION

An alliance, like a good friendship, takes effort. During the opening days of WWII, America viewed England as a friendship worthy of such effort. Franklin Roosevelt knew the coming visit by the British monarchs, King George VI, and Queen Elizabeth, was the perfect time to strengthen the trans-Atlantic friendship.

Consequently, the president pressed Ambassador William Bullitt on how best to meet the personal needs of the visiting monarchs. For the king's comfort, Bullitt suggested "two pillows...warm...light blankets, with silk covers...very soft eiderdown quilt, which can be accordion-pleated at the foot of the bed."[11]

The king would bring his own special cigarettes but would need a "dressing table with a triple mirror, high enough to enable contemplating oneself when standing."[12] The king's requirements continued, followed by an even more detailed catalog of the queen's needs. The comprehensive lists revealed the detail and preparation necessary to keep two eminent visiting dignitaries happy and an alliance strong.

Roosevelt's concern for small details, reflected in his insistence that the monarchs' accommodations be arranged with exactness and care, helped ensure the success of a valuable alliance. Similarly, extensive preparation by teachers is necessary for a successful school day. People sometimes note how effortless some instructors make teaching look, little understanding the countless details and hours of groundwork involved in preparing such a single lesson.

Good teachers make every student feel like a king and queen by maximizing effort, detail, and preparation. There are no accordion-pleated quilts or triple mirrors to welcome a student to class, but there should be a detailed plan that sparks a child's enthusiasm and interest for learning.

Question: What are examples of important details every teacher should address when creating a successful lesson?

STEP ON IT

It was August 2, 1941, and a clearly agitated FDR dictated a confidential letter to special assistant Wayne Coy demanding an expedited response to the Russian need for military assistance. Roosevelt was convinced that only immediate action by America could save Russia from being overrun by German aggressors.

Consequently, the president was even more frustrated by the slow response of American bureaucracy to his urgent request. He felt certain the Russians would interpret American inaction as having "been given the run-around" by the United States government.[13] He encouraged Coy to use "my full authority, use a heavy hand—act as a burr under the saddle and get things moving . . . Step on it!"[14] FDR's forceful actions ultimately enabled the Russians to not only hold on but eventually drive the Germans from their territory.

Institutional bureaucracy that slows progress is not exclusively a frustration for presidents like FDR. Too often, it is an obstacle to taking positive action in the school setting as well. When collective inertia stymies progress, it often takes a person willing to "act as a burr under the saddle" to get things moving.

When FDR wrote Coy, he was very exact in what he wanted done; likewise, when a school becomes moribund, a clear plan of action, with detailed steps and an explicit timetable, should be outlined and specific people be made accountable to carry out each phase. Students and parents must never feel they have been given the "run-around" by the very people who should be assisting them achieve academic success. As soon as a school becomes aware of a problem, it must find a way to "step on it" and help students conquer their academic foes.

Question: What is one area in which your school needs to "step on it?"

TIMELY ENCOURAGEMENT

In early April 1941, Britain had just sustained another devastating air raid from the Nazi regime of Adolph Hitler. The Germans believed their air campaign would quickly force the battered people of England to surrender. British Prime Minister Winston Churchill disagreed.

Demonstrating the pluck that would inspire the British people to victory, Churchill toured the most recent bombing, encouraging and reassuring the clearly stunned and demoralized population along the way. His efforts brought cheers from survivors. However, Churchill's private mood was less confident than his public appearances indicated.

At this low moment, President Roosevelt changed Churchill's dour mood by informing him that America was increasing its naval patrols, therefore helping identify the enemy "ships or planes" harassing England.[15] FDR's well-timed announcement bolstered Churchill and the British people, helping to pierce the glumness caused by the previous air assault.

The value of Roosevelt's timely encouragement to Churchill and the British people at a moment of increasing national despair cannot be underestimated. Likewise, educators should never fail to appreciate the power of a well-timed word or action in the life of a student or colleague facing a setback.

It is within every teacher's power to act by saving a discouraged student or peer from defeat. A positive note of encouragement, a phone call, or an offer to provide extra help on a difficult project are all acts of valuable and timely encouragement, mirroring the actions FDR provided Britain in its dire hour of need.

Question: To whom can you provide a timely word or act of encouragement?

TRANSFORMATIVE EVENTS

Frances Perkins, Franklin Roosevelt's secretary of labor, characterized FDR as a rather arrogant and self-righteous young politician, noting that he was "artificially serious of face, rarely smiling, with an unfortunate habit of throwing his head up, which, combined with his pince-nez [glasses] and great height, gave him the appearance of looking down his nose at most people."[16]

However, Roosevelt's confident demeanor quickly faded when he was infected with polio and its resulting paralysis. Perkins related how the years of suffering, as well as FDR's efforts to recover from the debilitating disease, led to a "spiritual transformation" that "purged his slight arrogance," leaving him "warmhearted, with new humility of spirit."[17] One result of this transformation was an unprecedented four terms as president.

Too often, tragedies like FDR's battle with polio strike during a school year. Misfortunes such as divorce, prolonged sickness, or a sports injury jeopardize a student's ability to complete a year successfully. Roosevelt's story of transformation from a self-absorbed politician into a warmhearted and personable leader demonstrates that students can overcome such adversity and even grow and thrive from life's difficulties.

While it is hard to see others suffer, it is okay to recognize that suffering sometimes refines and makes people better individuals. To ensure that such critical moments for students become transformative rather than debilitating events, educators should offer a listening ear, encouragement, comfort, and direction to the affected student. Your help may be the difference between paralysis and learning to move toward a richer and more successful life.

Question: How has adversity or tragedy in your life made you a better person or better teacher?

DEBRIEFING EXERCISE

Directions: Create a *word cloud* using ten words from the chapter on Franklin Roosevelt that best reflects your teaching approach. Record the words in the box below. Make the most important word the largest and then size each word accordingly. Then respond to the questions below.
Example:

> warmhearted
> transformation details loyal forthright optimistic encouragement discernment foresight actions

Questions:

1. What does your word choice reveal about you as an educator?
2. Have a peer identify the word they think most reflects you as an educator. Do you agree with their choice? Why or why not?

NOTES

1. Dole, Bob. *Great Presidential Wit*, New York: A Lisa Drew Book, 2001, page 54.
2. Ibid. Scottish people are traditionally known for their frugality, and therefore, by implication, FDR's dog, a Scottish terrier, is frugal, too.
3. Holy Bible, New International Version®, NIV® Copyright ©1973, 1978, 1984, 2011 by Biblica, Inc. https://www.biblegateway.com/passage/?search=Proverbs+17:22&version=NIV
4. McElvaine, Robert S. *The Depression and New Deal*, New York: Oxford University Press, 2000, pages 93-99.
5. Ibid.
6. Watkins, T. H. *The Great Depression: America in the 1930s*, Boston: Little, Brown and Company, 1993, pages 318-319.
7. Levering, Ralph, *The Cold War*, Yalta Plants Seeds of Cold War, http://www.realclearhistory.com/2012/02/04/yalta_plants_seeds_of_cold_war_1447.html, http://shs.westport.k12.ct.us/jwb/AP/ColdWar/Yalta.htm, Collections: February 4, 2012.
8. Mankowski, Diana, and Jose, Raissa, *MBC Flashback*, The 70th Anniversary of FDR's Fireside Chats, March 12, 1933, The Museum of Broadcast Communications, http://www.museum.tv/exhibitionssection.php?page=79.
9. Ibid.
10. Dorsett, Lyle W. *The Pendergast Machine*, Lincoln: University of Nebraska Press, 1968, pages 107, 132-135.
11. FDR 23: Letter, Amb. William C. Bullitt to FDR re: Preparations for the visit of the King and Queen of Great Britain, March 23, 1939, President's Secretary's Files; Diplomatic Correspondence; Great Britain, 1939 (Box 32), http://www.fdrlibrary.marist.edu/archives/significant-findingaid.html
12. Ibid.
13. FDR-32: Memorandum, FDR to Wayne Coy re: Aid to Russia, August 2, 1941, President's Secretary's Files: Diplomatic Correspondence: Russia, 1941 (Box 49). http://www.fdrlibrary.marist.edu/archives/significant-findingaid.html
14. Ibid.
15. Gilbert, Martin. *Churchill: A Life*, New York: Henry Holt and Company, 1991, page 696.
16. Perkins, Frances, The Roosevelt I Knew, serial installment in *Collier's: The National Weekly* for August 24, 1946, http://www.oldmagazinearticles.com/new_deal_labor_secretary_francis_perkins_memory_of_FDR_pdf
17. Ibid.

Chapter 8

Harry S. Truman

"I shall fight to end evils like this."
—Harry S. Truman

In an era in which physical strength and athleticism were valued, the need for thick and expensive glasses caused Truman to avoid sports; he played the piano instead. Equally unorthodox, Truman spied his future wife when he was only six and spent the next twenty-nine years pursuing the blue-eyed Bess Wallace, capturing her hand upon his return from the battlefields of France and World War I.

Ironically, a man known for his integrity, Truman entered the political profession with the assistance of the Kansas City political machine boss, Tom Pendergast. His first office was county judge; then senator; then, unexpectedly, vice president; and then, with the death of FDR, president. Many doubted Truman, he even doubted himself—but the doubt was unnecessary.

Before he was done, Truman would drop two atomic bombs and win a war, secure an election no one thought he could win, integrate the armed forces, recognize Israel, rebuild Western Europe and save it from Soviet control, protect Korea from communist domination, and establish a series of Cold War strategies that shaped American foreign policy for the next four decades. He did not need sports after all, as his administration proved to be one superb piano concerto.

CONFLICT MANAGEMENT

Americans like good wars, or at the very least, successful wars. Korea was no such war. Instead, it was an ugly conflict, featuring a prolonged stalemate and a ceasefire with no official end. Adding to the disheartening narrative was President Truman's decision to fire America's supreme commander in the Korean theater, Douglas MacArthur, for insubordination.

Truman did not want to dismiss MacArthur and went to considerable lengths to resolve their differences, even flying to Wake Island in the Pacific to meet the contentious general. The president hoped the meeting would provide him firsthand knowledge of the problems on the ground in Korea.

He hoped to minimize the time MacArthur spent away from the conflict, give him a chance to emphasize the strategic importance of the war, and, finally, provide an opportunity to demonstrate unity between him and the general. The meeting failed to achieve its objectives, and shortly thereafter MacArthur was fired.[1]

Although the president's attempts to reconcile with MacArthur failed, his efforts nonetheless provide a creditable outline for resolving disputes for today's educational setting. First, do not take any disciplinary action until you go directly to the person involved and hear his or her view on the matter.

Second, while resolving the conflict, create as little disruption to the classroom and school as possible. Third, emphasize the school's mission over personal preferences. And finally, work toward unity. Conflict and sustained differences almost always are disruptive to achieving academic success. Truman ultimately had to discipline MacArthur, but only after having first taken reasonable steps to resolve the conflict. Educators should do no less when facing their own troublesome personalities.

Question: What steps are you taking to alleviate conflict in your school?

IMPROBABLE ALLIANCE

"My dear Mr. President [Hoover]:--If you should be in Washington, I would be most happy to talk over the European food situation with you. Also, it would be a pleasure to me to become acquainted with you. Most sincerely HARRY S. TRUMAN"[2] Thus began one of the most unlikely political alliances and friendships in American political history.

It was a friendship vital to the salvation of post-WWII Europe, which faced growing chaos and starvation. Although Hoover had long been a target of partisan New Deal Democrats as the cause of the Great Depression, he had an indispensable talent for the present crisis—he knew how to help nations recover from the trauma of war.

Remarkably, as the United States Food Administrator during WWI, Hoover helped save millions of Europeans from starvation. Truman hoped to put these skills to work again, but members of both parties criticized the political alliance as unseemly, and many in Hoover's camp still felt bitter over his ill treatment by Democrats.

To the credit of both men, they overlooked past slights and current political risks for the good of their nation and the well-being of millions of starving Europeans. It was the beginning of an almost two-decade long partnership that benefited the many because they refused to be dissuaded by the few.[3]

Educators know all too well how pettiness and the refusal to work with peers due to real and imagined slights is not restricted to the political realm. It is easy to view academic rivals in a one-dimensional light, seeing only their flaws, while ignoring their strengths and virtues, which, if properly cultivated, could benefit a school greatly.

Like Truman and Hoover, it takes a great deal of humility to ignore past disagreements and offenses and forge a working relationship that places students and their welfare first. If national figures with long-standing political differences can work together, so can quarreling educators. Look at your peers, reach out, give grace, see the good, and make a difference together.

Question: Can you share an experience where you overcame personal differences with a colleague to achieve a common goal?

"JUST MAKING A SPEECH"

Harry Truman was a prolific letter writer, and no one received more attention from his pen than his wife, Bess. Although many of his letters to her contained trivialities about family, health, and relationships, Truman also filled many letters with political anecdotes that ranged from the serious to the humorous.

In one such letter, dated August 4, 1939, Truman detailed an event that occurred while he was still a senator and taking his turn presiding over the Senate. "Johnson of Colorado was making a speech. I rapped for order and requested that the Senate be quiet, so the Senator from Colorado could be heard—and the Senator from Colorado said he didn't want to be heard, he was just making a speech. I had to really call for order then."[4]

Although humorous, Senator Johnson's actions are all too familiar in some classrooms where assignments are created simply to keep students occupied, while failing to have an actual objective or purpose. Truman's tongue-in-cheek recounting of the senator's speech reflects a common criticism by students about the meaningless "busy work" they are often given to complete.

Handing out assignments void of clear objectives and real accountability eventually ceases to be humorous to students. They expect their efforts to be matched with legitimate homework or classwork that is worthy of mastering. Education should be fun, but it should never be a joke.

Question: How does a teacher ensure that his or her assignments are not "just making a speech" or busy work?

PRESS CONFERENCE SIMULATION

Press conferences are events in which presidents handle rapid-fire questions from an inquisitive and occasionally assertive press corps. During the summer of 1949, President Truman attended his 191st news conference.

Questions ranged from the building of a heavy water reactor, to the nomination of a new Supreme Court justice, to a rather impertinent question on whether the president was "afflicted with poweritis."[5]

Although some presidential responses were simple "no comments," his general practice was to respond to each inquiry with specific, albeit cautious replies.[6] Such spectacles reflect America's long tradition of an open and free society in which elected officials are expected to be able to defend their actions in an articulate and candid manner.

Simulating the give-and-take of a press conference through various classroom question-and-answer activities encourages students to go through the same rigors of preparation and research as Mr. Truman did for his encounters. Such question-and-answer exercises help equip students for future challenges such as job interviews and business negotiations which often require quick and effective responses.

When organizing a question-answer event, be sure to communicate to the class that *all* students should be prepared to ask and react to questions. Such preparation helps each student anticipate and plan for a greater variety of potential inquiries and responses, which further develops the ability to think critically.

This approach also diminishes the likelihood of teacher "poweritis," where the teacher controls all discussion and limits the development of crucial student thinking skills. Educators may be surprised by how a press conference approach can facilitate student movement beyond the "no comments" stage to the critical thinking stage of actually producing answers.

Question: What are the essential questions students should be asking and answering during your current unit?

REGULAR PEOPLE

Randall Jessee was a local newsman for *The Kansas City Star* and friend of the Truman family. He observed how extraordinary it was for the president and first lady, who "had everything in the world done for them for seven years," to eagerly return home to Independence and become regular people again.[7] It was as if they embraced the return to normalcy.

This became evident when Jessee witnessed Mrs. Truman "waiting tables and taking orders" at a social affair.⁸ Further confirmation came when Bess Truman revealed that the former president "washes dishes for her quite often and fixes his own breakfast."⁹ The president and his wife, Bess, had each returned to being "Citizen Truman," a remarkable metamorphosis and a model of the American democratic ideal.

Mr. Truman endeared himself to people like Randall Jessee because of his humble demeanor and his conduct that rejected any sense of entitlement. Truman was unique in that he never forgot that he was a citizen first and a president second. For educators, Truman's life is instructive on how humility and service often secure more esteem from students, peers, or parents than any title or position.

A good educator is not above doing hallway duty, cleaning up after a school event, sitting on a committee, or doing any other of a thousand minor tasks that need to be done if a school is to run efficiently. Every school needs more citizen-leaders like Truman who lead by humble example rather than by exalted title.

Question: What are some commonly neglected tasks at your school that educators are sometimes too proud to step up and do?

RESOLUTE

President Truman was only eleven days on the job and already a growing chorus within his administration was voicing concern that he was no Franklin Roosevelt. Adding to the apprehension was the concern an emboldened Soviet Union would take advantage of the inexperienced president during the conference on Europe's post-WWII fate.

Secretary of War Stimson glumly recorded in his diary, "I am very sorry for the President because he is new."¹⁰ Truman was determined to show the Soviets and his own advisors that he could be as tough a negotiator as FDR. Hence, while conferring with Soviet Foreign Minister Molotov over the future of Poland, Truman strongly conveyed that he expected the Russians to live up to all previous agreements made with President Roosevelt.

Molotov, unused to such blunt diplomatic talk, tersely responded, "I have never been talked to like that in my life." "Carry out your agreements and you won't get talked to like that," replied an equally curt Truman.¹¹ Any fear the president lacked resolve was removed at that moment.

Like Truman, new teachers are often compared unfavorably to their predecessors. Consequently, students and parents testing the novice teacher's aptitude for the job is not unusual. At such moments, consistent and firm resolve by the new instructor is necessary to establish credibility with his or her critics.

The new teacher must also exhibit competency by mastering the content, effective classroom management, and instructional expertise. Truman proved to the world he was up to the task of being president; the new teacher must resolutely prove he or she is up to the task of teaching, too.

Question: How have you demonstrated resolve when others have questioned your abilities?

RUSH TO DECISION

Albert Einstein questioned the wisdom of moving forward with the construction of the hydrogen bomb, fearing "General annihilation beckons" if completed.[12] President Truman, too, questioned the prudence of building a hydrogen bomb. Still, he was not convinced the dire warnings should stop all progress on the bomb's development.

He recalled how an earlier debate over America's role in protecting Greece had led to similar predictions of the "end of the world if we went ahead . . . The world didn't come to an end."[13] Also factoring into Truman's decision was Russia's development of its own bomb and its ever expanding military, the Communist takeover of China, and the sense that "temporizing was risky and might be fatal."[14]

In the end, the consequences of not developing a hydrogen bomb were too great to delay its development any longer. Consequently, Truman's press secretary announced to the world that America would "continue its work on all forms of atomic weapons, including the so-called hydrogen bomb or super bomb."[15]

Although few educators must grapple with the pressure President Truman faced during the debate on atomic weapon development, teachers and administrators often do face difficult decisions while burdened by time constraints. On such occasions, when haste is critical, educators should move forward on the decision as expeditiously as they can.

However, difficult decisions should involve input from multiple viewpoints, a thorough review of all aggravating and mitigating factors, and an analysis of possible intended and unintended consequences. Truman's admonition that "the world didn't come to an end" is a valuable reminder that even during a crisis, there is almost always more time for thoughtful reflection and marshaling advice before taking an action that might lead to later regret.

Question: When do you feel most pressured to make snap decisions, and how do you handle such situations?

THREE PROFESSIONS

Harry S. Truman identified three professions he believed were essential for successfully navigating life in the political arena—finance, farming, and the military. He personally fulfilled these objectives: working in several banking establishments in Kansas City; helping run the family farm in Grandview, Missouri; and, finally, performing military service in the National Guard during WWI and later in the Army Reserves.[16]

Although Truman did not graduate from college, his job experience provided a valuable education in finances, hard work, courage, and leadership, all skills that proved advantageous in his civic roles as judge, senator, vice president, and of course, president.

Truman's validation of learning by doing is a great reminder for educators that instruction should be experiential and not simply theoretical. After-school jobs, internships, community service projects, cooperative learning exercises, and an assortment of other hands-on approaches should be encouraged as part of a well-rounded education.

The experience of doing, with all its complications and obstacles, can provide invaluable lessons for students preparing for a complex future. Three different jobs served as instructional tutors for Truman, equipping the future president for the challenges ahead. Every teacher should make a list of character-molding and skill-inducing opportunities and share them with their students. After all, if a formal education were the only qualification to be a leader, Truman would never have become president.

Question: What are three jobs, activities, or books you would recommend as good preparation for a student's future?

TRANSFORMATIVE ACTION

Jackson County, Missouri, was a Confederate stronghold throughout most of the Civil War. Although the South lost the war, the vestiges of racial intolerance in the region continued long afterward, imparting to men like Harry Truman a negative view of black Americans.

However, an event at the end of WWII dramatically changed Truman's lifelong view of race: "My stomach turned over when I learned that Negro soldiers, just back from overseas, were being dumped out of army trucks in Mississippi and beaten. Whatever my inclinations as a native of Missouri might have been, as president I know this is bad. I shall fight to end evils like this."[17] Truman put his new worldview into practice by creating a Civil Rights

Commission to investigate such attacks and by ordering the integration of the armed forces.

Such radical changes were shocking to Southern sensibilities, and it quickly became evident that Truman's pro-civil rights position might cost him the Southern vote in the 1948 presidential election. In fact, many Southern states, led by Governor Strom Thurmond, did break away from Truman's Democrat party because of his emerging views on race.

When a reporter commented to Thurmond that the differences between Truman and his predecessor FDR on civil rights were minimal, Thurmond responded, "I agree. But Truman really means it."[18] Truman had moved from merely knowing what was right to doing what was right.

In today's modern schools, bullying, cheating, and drug and alcohol abuse are very real problems, even as racism was in the South of the 1940s. Helping students move from simply parroting school curriculum that labels such actions as wrong to truly believing it is wrong is a good first step.

But to complete the process, schools need to consistently encourage young adults to imitate Truman's bold actions by proactively creating a culture that does not tolerate such harmful behavior. Educators must join with students to first identify the problem, then own the problem, and then resolve to "fight to end" the problem. Confronting issues like bullying, cheating, and drugs cannot be limited to mere hallway posters or annual assemblies. In some classroom or hall is a child counting on a peer or teacher to "really mean it" and act.

Question: How is your school being transformative and proactive in the fight against bullying, cheating, or drug and alcohol abuse?

UNIFIED

WWII was a great victory for America's armed forces. However, the mission to defeat Berlin and Tokyo was often marred by infighting and a lack of coordination between the military branches that made the task more difficult than necessary.

Following the war, the Truman Administration made it a prime objective to unify the competing services into one cohesive organization. Secretary of War Stimson maintained that unification would eliminate the "wasteful opulence" inherent in having multiple independent branches of service.[19] The new system also established the office of secretary of defense[20] over a combined Army, Navy, and Air Force, thus deferring much of the president's supervisory burden. Finally, Truman hoped consolidation of the branches would help alleviate the distrust and jealousy revealed during the recent war.[21]

Since Truman reorganized the armed forces, they have operated more efficiently under the unified command of the secretary of defense, which is more than can be said for many schools where athletics, the arts, and academics ritually operate out of a spirit of shared envy and suspicion. A lack of coordination between academic programs and extracurricular programs often costs a school money and time, plus it diminishes the likelihood any one area will achieve excellence.

A strong administration that sets a standard of shared goals for the school, along with a faculty willing to recognize the value inherent in each facet of school life, is more likely to see a unified and positive workplace. Students deserve a school where distrust and jealousy between academics and extracurricular activities is replaced with a common vision to make all students successful.

Question: What can you do to promote greater unity between the various factions in your school?

DEBRIEFING EXERCISE

Truman stood up to the racial bullies of his era. Are you prepared to recognize and stop bullying at your school? The following is an activity to help you proactively address bullying in your school.

Directions. Identify the steps you would take to resolve an issue of bullying by numbering the action steps 1 - 10, with 1 being the first step you would take and 10 being the last step you would take.

_____Speak to the parents.
_____Identify everyone involved in the bullying incident.
_____Speak to the bully.
_____Follow up with the bullied student to see how they are doing.
_____Identify the student who is being bullied and talk to them.
_____Speak to the administration.
_____Involve other students.
_____Identify resources on bullying.
_____Verify that the issue is resolved.
_____Speak to the bullied student.

1. Discuss your ranking with your principal, your high school counselor, and your peers.
2. Would they order the steps differently? Why?
3. Is there an action that was not listed that you would add to the steps? Why?

NOTES

1. Truman, Harry S. *Memoirs by Harry S. Truman,* Volume Two: *Years of Trial and Hope,* Garden City, NY: Doubleday & Company, 1956, pages 364-368.
2. Letter, Harry S. Truman to Herbert Hoover, May 24, 1945, formally inviting Hoover to the White House to meet Truman and discuss the food situation in Europe. Papers of Herbert Hoover: Post-Presidential Files-Individual. http://www.trumanlibrary.org/hoover/internaltemplate.php?tldate=1945-05-24&groupid=5101&collectionid=hoover
3. Ibid.
4. Ferrell, Robert H., ed. *Dear Bess: The Letters from Harry to Bess Truman 1910-1959,* Columbia: University of Missouri Press, 1983, page 417.
5. The President's News Conference of July 28, 1949, pages 402-405, #166 of Public Papers of the President of the United States Harry S. Truman: Containing the Public Messages, Speeches, and Statements of the President, January 1 to December 31, 1949, Washington: United States Government Printing Office, 1964.
6. Ibid.
7. Dr. Philip C. Brooks, Oral History Interview with Mr. and Mrs. Randall S. Jessee, American Embassy, Copenhagen, Denmark, May 19, 1964, http://www.trumanlibrary.org/oralhist/jessee.htm
8. Ibid.
9. Ibid.
10. Moskin, Robert J. *Mr. Truman's War: The Final Victories of WWII and the Birth of the Postwar World,* New York: Random House, 1996, pages 80-83.
11. Ibid.
12. McCullough, David. *Truman,* New York: Simon & Schuster, 1992, pages 761-765.
13. Ibid.
14. Ibid.
15. Ibid.
16. Ferrell, Robert H. *Harry S. Truman: A Life,* Columbia: University of Missouri Press, 1994, page 23.
17. Keyes, Ralph. *The Wit and Wisdom of Harry Truman: A Treasury of Quotations, Anecdotes, and Observations,* New York: Gramercy Books, 1995, page 102.
18. Ibid.
19. Stimson, Henry L., and Bundy, McGeorge. *On Active Service in Peace and War,* New York: Harper and Brothers, 1948, pages 516-523.
20. Formerly the secretary of war.
21. Ibid.

Chapter 9

Dwight D. Eisenhower

"Optimism and pessimism are infectious."—Dwight D. Eisenhower

A West Point graduate, Eisenhower remained stateside during WWI, reluctantly watching peers gain valuable experience and acclaim. Although the young officer was not flashy, he was organizationally savvy, and the military noticed. When WWII commenced, it was Eisenhower elected to lead the invasion of North Africa, America's first major military operation.

Successful, he earned the ultimate command, directing the Allied invasion of Europe and the defeat of Nazi Germany. After a short stint as a university president, and as supreme commander of the Western alliance, NATO, Eisenhower was elected president. He presided over a time of great economic prosperity, the building of the interstate highway system, a space race, and a Cold War in which he skillfully managed to avoid a nuclear conflict. In the end, Eisenhower surpassed all his peers and reached the pinnacle of a successful officer, commander-in-chief.

COMMUNICATION, THE BEST MEDICINE

Polio was a horrendous disease. It killed hundreds of children each year and left thousands more crippled for life. Fear of the disease was almost as contagious as the ailment itself, as rumors spread rapidly, sparking panic in small and large communities across the country. The report of a new vaccine, introduced by the scientist Jonas Salk, delivered welcome relief, counteracting, and easing the worst fears of parents everywhere.[1] However, Eisenhower was troubled by the slow production of the vaccine.

He was even more alarmed that some doctors were telling frightened mothers that the government was slowing distribution of the life-giving serum. Eisenhower ordered his cabinet to quickly counteract this misinformation, requiring each cabinet official to make a public statement that the government was not hindering the immunization of children. He also insisted that debunking this false rumor would be a point of emphasis at his next press conference.² The president was determined to communicate truth as an antidote for fear.

Like Eisenhower, educators must accurately communicate to parents about important issues. Illness, bullying, unwelcome intruders, or any other perceived threat that might harm students all require prompt and accurate communication. When it comes to the safety and the well-being of children, parents will always be protective, sometimes reacting to unsubstantiated rumors out of fear for their child's security.

Educators should remember that although polio has been eradicated, the disease of misinformation and fear remains. Do not leave a vacuum of communication where misinformation and fear can breed. Provide clear and accessible answers as the antidote. Good communications should be like Salk's vaccine and spread relief to all parents.

Question: Where does your staff need to communicate better with parents?

DISCIPLINING A FAUBUS

Almost a hundred years after the Civil War, black Americans still faced discrimination and legalized segregation. Then, a sweeping Supreme Court ruling, *Brown v. Board of Education*, declared an end to such overt discrimination in public schools. However, southern culture said otherwise; led by the defiant Governor Orval Faubus, the National Guard was ordered to prevent all black students from entering Central High School in Little Rock, Arkansas.³

President Eisenhower, desirous of upholding federal law, while not alienating white southern voters, summoned Faubus for a meeting to tell him privately to end his unlawful actions. He bluntly told the governor, "The Federal government had assumed jurisdiction . . . the State would lose, and [he] did not want to see any Governor humiliated."⁴ Faubus refused to back down. This challenge to federal authority was too much. Eisenhower quickly cast aside his moderate approach, sending federal troops to force the uncooperative Faubus to obey the *Brown* decision and end segregation.⁵

Like Eisenhower, you need to let "your" classroom Faubus know that he or she cannot challenge your authority or disrupt your class. First, use nonverbal cues to end the troublesome behavior. To do this, you can catch the disruptive student's eyes with a stern look, or stand by the student while you lecture, or even quietly tap on the student's desk as you walk by. If required, hold a private meeting with the student to avoid embarrassing him or her.

The meeting should convey specific expectations the student must meet and the consequences he or she can anticipate if the student does not meet the conditions. If after a private meeting the problem persists, then a firmer and more public approach will become necessary to maintain authority.

Sentences, detentions, and contacting the parents are all appropriate steps to ensure that no one student can take away the right of other students to enter your class and learn.

Question: What steps do you take to discipline your classroom Faubus so that other students have the right to enter your class and learn?

FAVORITISM

Early in his career, General Eisenhower was often overshadowed by his more flamboyant and colorful contemporaries Douglas MacArthur and George Patton. Nevertheless, Eisenhower's "patient, clear, and logical" leadership and communication style enabled him to surpass both men in fame and accomplishment.[6] Adding to his success was his belief that great leaders must never show favoritism or set lax expectations for subordinates because it would lead to failure.

As Eisenhower explained, "Morale . . . withstands shocks, even disasters of the battlefield, but can be destroyed utterly by favoritism, neglect, or injustice."[7] Although he was a soldier's general, always attentive to the needs of his men, Eisenhower realized he could not "coddle" or show any unjust partiality toward certain men without undermining the morale and the effectiveness of the army.[8] He won a war with these principles.

Eisenhower emphasized the destructive nature of favoritism in the military. This practice is equally damaging in the field of education. In fact, overt favoritism toward some students, combined with persistent neglect and lack of encouragement for other students, can produce a toxic resentment that undercuts a school's overall educational success.

To avoid this problem, schools should develop and enforce high standards of excellence for everyone, where success is a result of effort and not preferential treatment. Not every student is equally gifted, but every student should be equally valued and equally challenged to work hard to achieve success.

Question: Where are you undermining student morale by demonstrating favoritism, neglect, or low expectations?

FLEXIBILITY

After two decades of big government growth, conservatives were ecstatic that an advocate of limited government, like Dwight Eisenhower, was once more at the helm. Then the president announced his plan to build a federal interstate highway system—one of the largest federal programs ever undertaken by the national government. Eisenhower knew this would be a difficult sell to his conservative colleagues at the federal and state level.

But sell it he did, arguing that the highway system would aid public commerce, meet America's ballooning population growth,[9] and provide a quick means to evacuate cities in case of a nuclear attack. Eisenhower further promised this would not be a big federal program, with the states bearing the majority of the financial commitment for the project.[10] It did not work out that way, however, as Congress recognized that the states could not bear such a large financial burden. Consequently, Congress reduced the states' obligation for the highway project from 70 percent to a mere 10 percent, an amount a flexible Eisenhower, eager to complete the task, accepted.[11,12]

President Eisenhower demonstrated flexibility by adjusting the cost-sharing formula to complete the federal highway system on time. Likewise, successful educators must be willing to alter their expectations when unforeseen changes to curriculum, class size, or objectives occur during the school year.

Coping with such adjustments is seldom easy. It requires a school culture willing to adapt to shifting conditions; a realistic understanding of the appropriate level of commitment and sacrifice required by all sides; and, when necessary, the flexibility to rebalance the level of responsibility between administration, faculty, parents, and students. Every educator needs to recognize that a key part of moving forward is a willingness to be flexible.

Question: Where can you be more flexible to help the school achieve its goals?

INFECTIOUS OPTIMISM

As WWII commenced, General Eisenhower took command of a new and untested American army. Though relatively inexperienced himself, he understood war's relentless nature and the need to counter its negative influence by modeling optimism whenever possible. He observed that "optimism and pessimism are infectious, and they spread more rapidly from the head downward than in any other direction."[13]

When Eisenhower became president, he continued this leadership approach by always wearing a ready smile and by modeling a positive attitude even through the difficult days of the Cold War and through his own personal struggles of a stroke and a heart attack.

Like Eisenhower, teachers should strive to be infectiously positive, replicating his advice to do your "best to meet everyone from general to private with a smile, a pat on the back and a definite interest in his problems." In the same way, resolve to be the teacher who demonstrates excitement for the curriculum, is quick to speak a word of encouragement, and acts daily to demonstrate a genuine concern for each student.

Then, watch as an infectious spirit takes hold in the classroom. As a leader at school, every educator can choose to create an affirmative culture, choose to smile, and choose to set the tone for a positive day of learning. Practice infectious optimism today.

Question: What is one way you are spreading optimism and one way you are spreading pessimism at your school?

NO

During the spring of 1960, Cold War[14] tension between the United States and the Soviet Union took a critical step toward peace as the two superpowers met at a summit to curb the escalating arms race. Suddenly, the peace overture was shaken with the news that an American U-2 reconnaissance spy plane had been shot down over Soviet airspace.[15] Nikita Khrushchev, the premier of Russia, demanded an apology and the renunciation of all future American attempts to spy on the Soviet Union.

President Eisenhower bluntly replied, "No," leading an enraged Khrushchev to storm out of the peace conference.[16] The president was unimpressed by Khrushchev's bluster. An apparently bemused Eisenhower confided to several of his top advisors how ridiculous such a request was, as everyone knew full-well that Russia would continue to spy on the United States regardless of the actions America took. The president believed that foreign intelligence operations could never be eliminated, and, therefore, each nation was responsible to battle and expose foreign espionage wherever it was found.[17]

Eisenhower's view of spying holds true for the practice of cheating in the classroom. Teachers can either approach cheating with the offended nature of a Khrushchev or with the cool resolve of an Eisenhower, accepting its existence and creating a countervailing strategy to defeat it and its considerable consequences.

A good way to limit the temptation to cheat is to require students taking a quiz or exam to clear their desks of all non-test-taking items except a cover sheet. Students should also be expected to put all papers away in their notebooks. Additionally, constant surveillance, while unwelcomed by Khrushchev and students alike, is the most important step a teacher can take to prevent cheating. Teachers must have a plan to defeat cheating even as nations necessarily must develop a plan to counteract spying.

Question: What is your plan to defeat cheating in your classroom?

PREMATURELY JUDGING STUDENTS

In America, it is not unusual to criticize and judge a president as a failure long before he leaves office. Often, such judgments solidify into fact, even though a president's motives and actions remain unknown for decades until his papers and classified documents are released. Such was the case in the Eisenhower presidency, with several historians maintaining that his administration was unremarkable, passive, and unimaginative. Eventually, as classified papers became available, historians like Fred Greenstein altered the view of Eisenhower's administration. Greenstein highlighted Eisenhower's efforts to end the Korean conflict and avoid a nuclear war with Russia as examples of a proactive and successful approach to governing.[18] Thanks to such research, the president's ranking among historians has risen dramatically.

Prejudging people is not just an issue with presidential critics and historians. Too often educators fall into the same trap, prematurely judging students based on one incident, the unfounded reports of other teachers, or the tendency to confuse student immaturity with student ability. One should remember that students who are often identified as troublemakers, poor learners, or lazy, frequently turn out to be very successful when properly mentored and given time to mature.

Historians must patiently wait for the declassification of presidential papers; likewise, teachers need patience when training young people. Every student should be taught, disciplined, and inspired as an individual who has the potential to succeed. As the life of Eisenhower proved, there is often more to an individual than initial appearance.

Question: What are some common examples of teachers and administrators prejudging students?

TEACHING MOMENTS

Eisenhower, one of America's greatest generals and statesmen, had a recurring character issue he spent a lifetime battling—anger. On one occasion, as a young boy, he grew so irate over not being allowed to go trick-or-treating "he rushed outside and began pounding the trunk of a tree with his bare fists. He sobbed and pounded until his fists were a raw bleeding mass of torn flesh."[19] Finally, his father had to physically restrain him and remove him to his bedroom where he continued to cry for another hour.

As he calmed down, his mother bandaged and soothed his battered hands. After a time, she gently reminded her son of the proverb, "He that conquereth his own soul is greater than he who taketh a city." She explained the destructive nature of anger and why he needed to conquer it before it conquered him. When Eisenhower was seventy-six years old, he wrote, "I have always looked back on that conversation as one of the most valuable moments of my life."[20]

Eisenhower credits his mother with giving him the key to anger management, and because he followed her advice, he enjoyed an extraordinary military and political career. Education is full of similar mentoring opportunities. As teachers observe student character flaws such as cheating, disrespect, bullying, and so on, they should take such "moments of life" and use them as opportunities to inspire students to "conquer their own souls." Cities wait to be conquered, but students might need a little well-timed advice, correction, and encouragement to get there.

Question: How are you taking advantage of the "moments of life" to impart life changing advice?

THE EMPATHETIC TEACHER

In the late 1940s, the black baseball player Jackie Robinson led the drive to integrate baseball. A decade later, a retired Robinson attended the Summit Meeting of Negro Leaders where he heard President Eisenhower urge black Americans to be patient with the slow progress of integration. The hard-charging Robinson, believing the president's speech showed a lack of understanding and empathy for the plight of black Americans, responded with a stinging letter to Eisenhower:

"On hearing you say this, I felt like standing up and saying, 'Oh no! Not again.'. . . As the chief executive of our nation, I respectfully suggest that you unwittingly crush the spirit of freedom in Negroes by constantly urging forbearance."[21] Robison respectfully, but forcefully, called the nation's chief executive to have greater empathy for the plight of black America.

As a soldier, Eisenhower had felt the pain of war and could relate to veterans who had experienced its enduring wound, but with the ache of bigotry, he had less empathy or understanding. Into this vacuum stepped Jackie Robinson, who wanted the president to understand and appreciate the bite of racism that black America, and he personally, had experienced. Similarly, teachers need to be aware of the struggles students face, such as time-consuming athletic practices and games, job responsibilities, family obligations, and any of a long variety of other pressing issues.

Showing empathy for such concerns does not mean lowering expectations and standards; instead, it means taking the time to look at the whole student and the forces shaping his or her academic performance, and then responding to the student accordingly. Eisenhower clearly struggled to understand and empathize with the plight of black Americans; teachers should not make the same mistake with their students.

Question: What steps can you take to develop better understanding and empathy for your students?

WORTHY AMBITION

A perpetual question in almost every profession is how to measure success. The military answered this question by demanding that officers and enlisted men work hard to earn their promotions and move up the chain of command. Eisenhower, one of America's premier soldiers, practiced an additional benchmark: always do your best.

Correspondingly, he wrote, "My ambition in the army was to make everybody I worked for regretful when I was ordered to other duty."[22] Not content with merely rising through the ranks, Eisenhower wished to be indispensable at each level of service and, upon promotion, missed.[23] The young officer's approach to work led to the ultimate promotion: commander-in-chief of the United States.

Like Eisenhower, an educator should be so effective that administrators, parents, and students will regret his or her transfer to "other duty." For instance, administrators appreciate the teacher who faithfully shows up for duties, works to improve his or her teaching knowledge and skills, and volunteers without grumbling. Parents value the teacher who communicates regularly, sets high standards, and shows real interest in their child's well-being.

As for students, they welcome the teacher who maintains good classroom control, demonstrates a passion for his or her subject matter, and exhibits real concern for each pupil. Such qualities make a teacher indispensable. It is natural to seek personal recognition and promotion; it is nobler to live a life worthy of being missed. Like Eisenhower, every teacher should make this his or her ambition.

Question: What actions could you take today that would cause people to regret if you left tomorrow?

DEBRIEFING EXERCISE

1. What are three worthy ambitions (vision, goals, purposes, etc.) you try to instill in your students?
2. How are these ambitions incorporated into your curriculum?
3. How do you model these ambitions to your students?

NOTES

1. Digital Documents and Photographs Project: Jonas Salk and the Polio Vaccine, www.eisenhower.archives.gov, accessed 6/29/10.
2. Minutes of Cabinet Meeting on the Salk vaccine, April 29, 1955 [DDE's Papers as President, Cabinet Series, Box 5, Cabinet Meeting of 4/29/55].
3. Digital Documents and Photographs Project: Civil Rights: The Little Rock School Integration Crisis, www.eisenhower.archives.gov, accessed 6/28/10.
4. Diary - notes dictated by President Eisenhower on October 8, 1957 concerning meeting with Governor Faubus at Newport, Rhode Island, September 14, 1957 [DDE's Papers as President, Administration Series, Box 23, Little Rock Ark (2)].
5. Digital Documents and Photographs Project: Civil Rights: The Little Rock School Integration Crisis, www.eisenhower.archives.gov, accessed 6/28/10.
6. Ambrose, Stephen E. *Eisenhower: Soldier and President*, New York: Simon and Schuster, 1990, page 55.
7. Ibid.
8. Ibid.
9. Digital Documents and Photographs Project: Interstate Highway System, www.eisenhower.archives.gov, accessed 6/30/10.
10. Message to the Congress regarding highways, February 22, 1955.
11. Letter from Roger Jones to President Eisenhower concerning the Federal-Aid Highway Construction Program, June 28, 1956.
12. Meeting of April 6, 1960. regarding the Interstate Highway Program, April 8, 1960.
13. Ambrose, *Eisenhower*, page 82.
14. "A struggle over political differences (as of two nations) carried on by methods short of war and usually without breaking off diplomatic relations," Merriam-Webster Word Central, Student Dictionary, http://www.wordcentral.com/cgi-bin/student?book=Student&va=cold%20war, retrieved 3/2/18.
15. Digital Documents and Photographs Project: The U-2 Spy Plane Incident, www.eisenhower.archives.gov, accessed 6/28/10.
16. Memorandum of Conference with the President on 5/15/60, dated May 16, 1960 regarding U-2 and summit conference [DDE's Papers as President, DDE Diary Series, Box 50, Staff Notes May 1960 (1)].
17. Ibid.
18. Greenstein, Fred I. *Profiles of U.S. Presidents: Dwight D. Eisenhower.* www.presidentprofiles.com, accessed 6/28/10.
19. Ambrose, *Eisenhower*, page 18-19.
20. Ibid.
21. Letter from Jackie Robinson to President Dwight D. Eisenhower, White House Central Files Box 731, File: OF-142-A-3, Dwight D. Eisenhower Library, National Archives and Records Administration.
22. Ambrose, *Eisenhower*, page 54.
23. Ibid.

Chapter 10

Ronald Reagan

"... the courage to face our faults and the strength to correct our errors."
—Ronald Reagan

Reagan began as a sports broadcaster on radio, eventually embarking on a Hollywood career that included fifty-three movies, with stints of military service in between. He famously became a Republican in the early 1960s, arguing he had not left the Democrat party, they had left him. He became a two-term governor of California, proving he was more than a Hollywood actor.

Elected president in 1980, he introduced steep tax cuts called Reaganomics, which sparked a moribund economy, he survived an assassination attempt, restored American confidence following the troubling 1970s, and used an arms race to weaken the Soviet Union, which collapsed a few short years later. Reagan was an effective communicator as a broadcaster and as an actor, but it was only as president that he became known as the "Great Communicator," leaving office as one of the most popular presidents of the twentieth century.

CHANGING THE NARRATIVE

Moving into his second term, President Reagan, who described the Soviet Union as the "Evil Empire," was confronted by a new Russian leader, Mikhail Gorbachev. Gorbachev promised to change the aggressive perception of his country by withdrawing from Afghanistan, a country Russia had invaded, and by slowing the American-Soviet arms race. Even with these actions, the negative view of the new Russian president would not be an easy narrative to break, as leading American publications alternately referred to Gorbachev as a "deceptive, brutal Stalinist" and as "vintage Stalin."[1]

British Prime Minister Margaret Thatcher was one of the first leaders to counter this story line, insisting that Gorbachev was a man America could work with and that she personally liked him. Thatcher's view, coupled with Mrs. Reagan's insistence that her husband soften his hard-line stance toward the Soviets, moved Reagan to embrace a new approach of cooperation and negotiation with Gorbachev and with the Soviet Union.[2]

Not unlike Gorbachev, students sometimes carry an undesirable narrative based on past actions. Previous negative conduct such as disrespect, bullying, or laziness often overshadows a student's profession of reform, making it difficult to rewrite how he or she is seen by teachers. To change such a negative opinion, it takes a respected person in the Thatcher mold to create a new perception of the student or a Nancy Reagan-like educator to insist a student be given a fresh opportunity to succeed. Ultimately, creating a new narrative requires a student willing to change his or her negative behavior and an educator willing to invest in and take a chance on the reformed student.

Question: Can you describe a student you are currently teaching who might achieve success if he or she is given the chance to break away from his or her current unfavorable narrative?

CHASTENED, BUT STRONGER

On a somber afternoon in 1986, Ronald Reagan stood in the Rose Garden, unenviably delivering the Presidential Commission's conclusions on the Space Shuttle Challenger accident, an event in which seven astronauts died shortly after liftoff. Reagan was proud of how the commission handled its "painful duty."[3]

He believed it was necessary to thoroughly examine, in an "unfettered" manner, what went wrong so that it would not happen again.[4] Only a "free and open society," he continued, has "the courage to face our faults and the strength to correct our errors."[5] Reagan believed that such a country, so "chastened," would be less likely to repeat such mistakes, and "although the lessons of failure are hard, they are often the most important on the road to progress."[6]

Reagan's insights into addressing the failure of the Space Shuttle Challenger are relevant for the struggling educator. Teachers need "courage to face our faults and . . . strength to correct our errors." As President Reagan recognized, people cannot make progress unless they first thoroughly examine why they are failing and then correct their shortcomings.

Whether it is poor classroom management, difficulty communicating concepts to students, or the inability to manage multiple responsibilities, every teacher faces disappointment. Such letdowns should not be the end but, rather, the beginning of being a better teacher. It takes courage to correct deficiencies after being chastened by failure, but it is the only true path to progress.

Question: When have you been chastened by failure, admitted it, and created a plan to fix it?

DISTRIBUTING POWER FAIRLY

One of the ongoing quarrels during the Reagan era was how best to distribute money to the states. Reagan believed the power to conduct such operations should ultimately reside with state and local governments, an idea that often brought him into conflict with speaker of the House, Tip O'Neill. The president accused the speaker of being a classic New Dealer who wished to relegate "the states to administrative districts of the Federal government."[7]

The speaker countered that it was a matter of separation of powers and that "Congress would be abdicating its responsibility" if it let the executive branch determine how money should be allocated to the states.[8] Both sides grudgingly held to their views, believing that their methods for distributing federal money to the states was correct.

Power struggles, like the one that occurred during the Reagan Administration, are all too common in the educational realm between teachers and administrators. By clearly defining expectations and boundaries for both parties, such educational conflicts can be diminished.

Administrators must have enough authority to ensure that teachers are providing a safe and effective learning environment, while at the same time avoiding administrative micromanagement of teachers that can stifle their styles of teaching and their creativity. Whether finalizing difficult issues like curriculum, extracurricular duties, or pay and benefits, input and compromise between teachers and administrators is necessary if the members of a school wish to successfully move forward together.

Question: What can you do to help your school resolve disputes over power so that you can successfully move forward together?

"DO YOU KNOW?"

It was a mere eighteen years after John F. Kennedy was assassinated that America faced national tragedy again. This time the outcome would be different, as Ronald Reagan, shot shortly after delivering a speech at a local hotel, made a remarkably quick recovery. However, as detailed in the book *Rawhide Down*, the survival of President Reagan was far more tenuous than most Americans realized at the time. Even the president did not fully comprehend what had transpired.

When Reagan's surgeon Dr. David Gens asked him, "Mr. President, do you know what happened?" Reagan replied, "No." Gens then explained the gravity of the situation to the president, informing him that his lung was punctured and was filling with blood and losing air. Next, the doctor detailed the steps necessary to restore the president. Even then, Reagan needed further encouragement from the technician monitoring his vitals who assured him, "You are doing fine." He did do fine, returning to his residence at 1600 Pennsylvania Avenue only twelve days after the attempt on his life.[9]

In the chaos that ensued after the assassination attempt on Reagan's life, Dr. Gens took an action that too often educators forget to do: he detailed both the problem and the solution so that the patient knew exactly what had to be done to see improvement. Students struggling academically need similar detail and assurance. They need help identifying the source of their academic problem as well as specific, measurable solutions to fix their malady. Those faltering academically also need reassurance from their teacher, like the encouragement President Reagan received from the young technician. Such a student might need words of assurance like, "Work hard, follow the plan, you will do fine." A good teacher, like a good doctor, is best equipped to identify the problem, the solution, and the right level of encouragement to meet the challenge.

Question: Can you identify a student who does not know why he or she is failing and help him or her create a plan for success?

PEOPLE, NOT BUREAUCRACY

Ronald Reagan came into office vowing to "curb the size and influence of the federal establishment."[10] He asserted, "All of us should remember that the federal government is not some mysterious institution comprised of buildings, files, and paper. The people are the government."[11]

To make his vision a reality, Reagan made the government more responsive to the people by reducing the exchange of paperwork between businesses and government agencies. He also decreased the wait time for the average citizen to receive his or her Social Security card or passport from forty-nine days and forty-three days, respectively, to ten days. Reagan "believed that the government should work for the people, not the other way around."[12]

Schools, like the federal government, can quickly become nothing more than an unfeeling bureaucracy, frustrating and alienating the very parents and students they are designed to serve. When people feel their school has become a "mysterious institution comprised of buildings, files, and paper," it takes a Reagan-like administrator or teacher to make a difference.

Such a leader will eliminate unneeded bureaucracy and return the school to its primary function—instruction provided by responsive and caring educators. School employees should make sure parents and students feel like there is a person behind every email, phone call, memo, or school directive. It should never be a mystery whether the administration and staff care.

Question: Where has bureaucracy replaced direct, personal instruction and communication in your school?

PREPARATION, NOT MAGIC

Presidents often invite championship sports teams to the White House to recognize their accomplishments. Ronald Reagan practiced this tradition in 1985 by welcoming the NCAA basketball champion Villanova Wildcats to a Rose Garden ceremony. The event was particularly rewarding because no one expected such an underrated "Cinderella Team" to win.[13]

Reagan, however, did not believe the Cinderella label fit, believing it took "hard hours of preparation . . . to turn a group of tremendous individual players into a team that will go down in the history books."[14] Reagan emphasized that it was thorough preparation and rigorous effort that enabled Villanova to achieve success, rather than simply good fortune or "magic."[15]

The president's insight that teams succeed through hard work and preparation, rather than simple luck or magic, is instructive for becoming a winning teacher, too. Students and parents often recognize effective teachers, but incorrectly diagnose why they are successful, mistaking good lessons, effective classroom control, and engaged students as simply good fortune.

For the successful teacher, magic moments in the classroom come by thoroughly researching and planning each lesson, setting clear expectations for behavior, and investing time into each student. Consequently, a Cinderella fairy-tale-like classroom experience may come true, but usually only because of hard work and preparation.

Question: What does hard work and preparation look like for a successful teacher?

PRESIDENTIAL HOMEWORK

Even presidents do homework. Ronald Reagan was no exception to the rule. In diary entries, Reagan recorded how he "spent both afternoons doing homework,"[16] had "a quiet day at home catching up on homework,"[17] and "stayed in working all day [on] homework."[18]

The president enjoyed these times of preparation remarking, "Another busy day. I hate those days where I have one meeting right after the other with no time to collect my thoughts between meetings."[19] Whether prepping for a meeting on the Sinai in Egypt or trying to understand the military capability of the Soviet Union, Reagan always saw the critical need to do his homework and be prepared.

Ronald Reagan's diary reveals a leader who believed doing homework was critical to his success, a lesson every educator should copy to create a successful classroom experience. Effective teachers establish a routine of setting aside time to do their homework and prepare for each class. Success comes when teachers take time to identify the next day's objectives, thoroughly research the topic, and outline a plan of action that will both inform and engage students on the subject. Homework isn't just for presidents, or even students, it is for teachers, too.

Question: How much homework time is necessary to be an effective teacher in the classroom?

RECAPPING THE MEETING

Wrestling over common concerns of trade, the border, and overall increased cooperation, President Ronald Reagan and Mexican President Miguel de La Madrid met face to face in 1983. The meeting between the two heads of state was productive. They successfully negotiated trade agreements, agreed to address the growing drug traffic along the border, and gave "special attention to cultural exchange as well as scientific and technical cooperation between Mexico and the United States."[20]

As the meeting concluded, their staff recognized and reviewed several areas of agreement, as well as identified areas for possible future joint ventures.[21] By recapping the meeting, the two nations confirmed agreement on the results and laid the groundwork for future interaction between the neighboring countries.

Teachers meeting with parents over a struggling student or administrators mentoring a struggling teacher can learn from Reagan's approach to diplomacy. By taking time to recap discussions, each side can confirm or reject the stated conclusion. While reviewing the agreement, it is critical both parties agree on the source of the problem and its solution.

Be mindful when recapping a meeting to avoid misunderstandings that might keep the participants from moving forward together. Practicing the process of summarizing or recapping every meeting helps bring immediate resolution to a conflict and builds mutual trust to address future areas of disagreement. Not restating the conclusion of a meeting risks more conflict and the need for another meeting. Recap or come back.

Question: How might you recap a meeting with a subordinate, student, or parent differently?

SUCCESSFUL COLLABORATION

During the 1980s, the western hemisphere increasingly became a battleground between Communist forces and the United States. One such battleground was Nicaragua, where the Communist Sandinistas quickly gained a foothold. Fearing their growing power, President Reagan asked Congress to provide a $100 million aid package to the Contras, an anti-Communist military force. Congress said no.

Desperate, the Reagan Administration circumvented Congress by secretly authorizing the sale of weapons to Iran, an enemy of the United States. The administration hoped the arms deal would provide money for the Contras, improve America's strained relations with Iran, and free hostages held by Iranian sponsored terrorists. This failed policy became known as the Iran-Contra Scandal.

In contrast to Nicaragua, President Reagan took a different and very open and collaborative approach confronting terrorism in Libya, reaching out to leaders of both parties and gaining their consent for a military strike.[22] In the end, the highly secretive Iran-Contra action became one of Reagan's greatest failures, while the highly collaborative military assault against Libya became a noted success of his administration.

When a secretive and insular school environment develops, comparable to Reagan's failed approach in the Iran-Contra affair, negative consequences often ensue. For instance, when administrators make decisions without teacher input, it can lead to resentment and recrimination by teachers excluded from choices that directly affect them.

Similarly, when a teacher conceals his or her professional struggles from the administration, he or she undermines the administration's ability to help the teacher resolve the problem. In both instances, the vital band of trust is broken. Ultimately, secrecy leads to isolation and failure, while collaboration builds trust and mutual support that leads to success.

Question: In what area should your school increase its openness and level of collaboration?

"TRUST, BUT VERIFY"

As the years pass, it is easy to forget the dread a possible nuclear exchange between the United States and the Soviet Union evoked. To avoid such a possibility, Ronald Reagan met Soviet leader Mikhail Gorbachev in Reykjavik, Iceland. The president, who had referred to the Soviet Union as "the focus of evil in the modern world," hoped to fashion a new relationship by deescalating the arms race.[23]

However, Reagan was not naive and knew that any agreement would need accountability. Deftly using a Russian adage, "trust, but verify," Reagan insisted that there be a mechanism for ensuring compliance through inspection.[24] Thus, Reagan clearly outlined that sustained trust had to be earned through continuous and tangible verification.

President Reagan's expression, "trust, but verify," works not only for "evil empires" but in the lives of students, too. One of the great moments in the life of any educator is when he or she witnesses a student with a history of disciplinary issues making a choice to go in a new and a positive direction.

Accordingly, there is a desire to reward such a choice by giving the student either greater freedom or greater responsibility. Both require increased trust. However, as President Reagan understood, trust is earned, and, therefore, students should meet tangible, verifiable goals to demonstrate that their new course is authentic.

Question: What are some practical ways to demonstrate trust toward students while verifying they deserve the trust given to them?

DEBRIEFING EXERCISE

Reagan often did homework to prepare for meetings with other leaders and to prepare for the task of being president. If you were assigning homework to make yourself a better teacher, what would you assign . . .

1. To read? Why?
2. To visit (museum, national park, etc.)? Why?
3. To attend (conference, seminar, lecture, etc.)? Why?
4. To acquire (posters, technology, artifacts, etc.)? Why?
5. To eliminate (Sometimes homework is just busy work and distracts you from the real objective.)? Why?

NOTES

1. Wilentz, Sean. *The Age of Reagan: A History 1974–2008*, New York: HarperCollins Publishers, 2008, pages 246–247, 250–251.
2. Ibid.
3. Ronald Reagan Presidential Library & Museum. , Remarks on Receiving the Final Report of the Presidential Commission on the Space Shuttle Challenger Accident, June 9, 1986, http://www.reagan.utexas.edu/archives/speeches/publicpapers.html#.

Uotyo2znbIU, http://www.reagan.utexas.edu/search/speeches/speech_srch.html, dtSearch Web Search, retrieved 11/19/13.

4. Ibid.
5. Ibid.
6. Ibid.
7. The Ronald Reagan Presidential Foundation and Library, Home, Ronald Reagan, White House Diary, Thursday, June 18, 1981, http://www.reaganfoundation.org/white-house-diary.aspx, retrieved 6/18/2013.
8. Ibid.
9. Wilber, Del Quentin. *Rawhide Down: The Near Assassination of Ronald Reagan*, New York: Henry Holt and Company, 2011, pages 3-4, 114, and 140-141.
10. The Ronald Reagan Presidential Foundation & Library. Reagan Quotes, Inaugural Address 1/20/1981, http://www.reaganfoundation.org/the-presidency.aspx, retrieved 11/15/2013.
11. The Ronald Reagan Presidential Foundation & Library. Reagan Quotes, News Conference 1/29/1981, http://www.reaganfoundation.org/the-presidency.aspx, retrieved 11/15/2013.
12. The Ronald Reagan Presidential Foundation & Library. President Reagan's Domestic Policy: A More Perfect Union, http://www.reaganfoundation.org/the-presidency.aspx, retrieved 11/15/2013.
13. Remarks Congratulating the Villanova University Wildcats on Winning the National Collegiate Athletic Association Basketball Championship, April 4, 1985. The Ronald Reagan Presidential Foundation & Library, http://www.reaganfoundation.org/; Public Papers of Ronald Reagan, April 1985, http://www.reagan.utexas.edu/archives/speeches/publicpapers.html#.UksCz2wo4dW. http://www.reagan.utexas.edu/archives/speeches/1985/40485a.htm.
14. Ibid.
15. Ibid.
16. The Ronald Reagan Presidential Foundation & Library. REAGANFOUNDATION.ORG/WHITE-HOUSE-DIARY, http://www.reaganfoundation.org/WHITE-HOUSE-DIARY.aspx, October 12, 1981.
17. The Ronald Reagan Presidential Foundation & Library. REAGANFOUNDATION.ORG/WHITE-HOUSE-DIARY, http://www.reaganfoundation.org/WHITE-HOUSE-DIARY.aspx, October 25, 1981.
18. The Ronald Reagan Presidential Foundation & Library. REAGANFOUNDATION.ORG/WHITE-HOUSE-DIARY, http://www.reaganfoundation.org/WHITE-HOUSE-DIARY.aspx, October 31, 1981.
19. The Ronald Reagan Presidential Foundation & Library. REAGANFOUNDATION.ORG/WHITE-HOUSE-DIARY, http://www.reaganfoundation.org/WHITE-HOUSE-DIARY.aspx, October 14, 1981.
20. The Ronald Reagan Presidential Foundation & Library, Public Papers of Ronald Reagan, August 1983, http://www.reaganfoundation.org/; http://www.reagan.utexas.edu/archives/speeches/1983/81483e.htm. Joint Communique Following Discussions with President Miguel de la Madrid Hurtado of Mexico, August 14, 1983.
21. Ibid.

22. Reeves, Richard. *President Reagan: The Triumph of Imagination*, New York: Simon & Schuster, 2005, pages 313–316.

23. Ronald Reagan, Address to the National Association of Evangelicals ("Evil Empire Speech"). Voices of Democracy: The U.S. Oratory Project. University of Maryland, College Park, March 8, 1983, retrieved April 19, 2015.

24. Beschloss, Michael. *Presidential Courage: Brave Leaders and How They Changed America 1789–1989*, New York: Simon and Schuster Paperbacks, 2007, pages 309–310.

Bibliography

Abbott, W. W., et al., eds. *The Papers of George Washington, Presidential Series*, Vol. 4 (Dorothy Twohig, volume editor). Charlottesville: University Press of Virginia, 1993. The original autograph letter addressed to and signed by is located in the Papers of the Continental Congress in the National Archives in Washington, DC, item 78. http://gwpapers.virginia.edu/documents/goddard/index.html

Ambrose, Stephen E. *Eisenhower Soldier and Statesman*. New York: Simon and Schuster, 1990.

Ambrose, Stephan E. *Undaunted Courage*. USA: Simon and Schuster, 1996.

American President: A Reference Resource, Hoover's New Approach. http://millercenter.org/academic/americanpresident/hoover/essays/biography/4, Miller Center, University of Virginia, HISTORY.POLICY. IMPACT. Retrieved 6/13/2013.

Bailey, Thomas A. *A Diplomatic History of the American People*. New York: F. S. Crofts & Co., third edition 1947, sixth edition 1958.

Bernard, Kenneth A. *Lincoln and the Music of the Civil War*, pages 1–9. http://www.abrahamlincolnsclassroom.org/Library/newsletter.asp?ID=29&CRLI=109&searchWord=Lincoln%20%And%20%The%20%Music%20%Of%20%The%20%Civil%20%War. Retrieved 9/17/2012.

Beschloss, Michael. *Presidential Courage: Brave Leaders and How They Changed America 1789–1989*. New York: Simon and Schuster Paperbacks, 2007.

Boaz, David. *The Man Who Would Not Be King*. Cato Institute. http://www.cato.org/publications/commentary/man-who-would-not-be-king. 2/20/06, retrieved 9/24/15

Book of James. In *The Comparative Study Bible*. Michigan: The Zondervan Corporation, 1984.

Bowen, Catherine Drinker. *John Adams and the American Revolution*. Boston: Little, Brown and Company, 1950.

Brodie, Fawn M. *Thomas Jefferson: An Intimate History*. New York: Norton & Company, Inc., 1974.

Brookhiser, Richard. *George Washington on Leadership*. New York: Basic Books, 2008.

Brooks, Philip C., Dr. Oral History Interview with Mr. and Mrs. Randall S. Jessee. American Embassy, Copenhagen, Denmark, May 19, 1964. http://www.trumanlibrary.org/oralhist/jessee.htm

Collected Works of Abraham Lincoln. Volume 6: *Lincoln, Abraham, 1809–1865.* http://quod.lib.umich.edu/cgi/t/text/text-idx?c=lincoln;rgn=div1;view=text;idno=lincoln6;node=lincoln6%3A314

Works of Abraham Lincoln. Volume 8: *Lincoln, Abraham, 1809-1865.* To William P. Fessenden, September 16, 1864, Annotation: [1] Parke-Bernet Catalog 905, December 1-2, 1947, No. 278. http://quod.lib.umich.edu/l/lincoln/lincoln8/1:19

Diary - notes dictated by President Eisenhower on October 8, 1957 concerning meeting with Governor Faubus at Newport, Rhode Island, September 14, 1957 [DDE's Papers as President, Administration Series, Box 23, Little Rock Ark (2)].

Digital Documents and Photographs Project: Civil Rights: The Little Rock School Integration Crisis. www.eisenhower.archives.gov. Accessed 6/28/10.

Digital Documents and Photographs Project: Interstate Highway System. www.eisenhower.archives.gov. Accessed 6/30/10.

Digital Documents and Photographs Project: Jonas Salk and the Polio Vaccine. www.eisenhower.archives.gov. Accessed 6/29/10.

Digital Documents and Photographs Project: The U-2 Spy Plane Incident. www.eisenhower.archives.gov. Accessed 6/28/10.

Dole, Bob. *Great Presidential Wit.* New York: A Lisa Drew Book, 2001.

Dorsett, Lyle W. *The Pendergast Machine.* Lincoln: University of Nebraska Press, 1968.

Ellis, Gordon J. *His Excellency: George Washington.* New York: Vintage Books, A Division of Random House, Inc., 2004.

Ellis, Joseph J. *Founding Brothers: The Revolutionary Generation.* New York: Vintage Books, A Division of Random House, Inc., 2000.

Epstein, Daniel Mark. *The Lincolns: Portrait of a Marriage.* New York: Ballantine Books, 2008.

Everett, Marshall, and others. *Roosevelt's Thrilling Experiences in the Wilds of Africa and Triumphal Tour of Europe.* A. Hamming, 1910.

Evolution of the Conservation Movement, 1850–1920. http://memory.loc.gov

Extracts from Thomas Jefferson's Hints to Americans Traveling in Europe. Papers of Thomas Jefferson Retirement Series Digital Library. www.monticello.org, 6/30/2010.

Extracts from Thomas Jefferson's letter to Brissot de Warville. Papers of Thomas Jefferson Retirement Series Digital Library. www.monticello.org, 6/30/2010.

FDR-23: Letter, Amb. William C. Bullitt to FDR re: preparations for the visit of the King and Queen of Great Britain, March 23, 1939, President's Secretary's Files; Diplomatic Correspondence; Great Britain, 1939 (Box 32). http://www.fdrlibrary.marist.edu/archives/significant-findingaid.html

FDR-32: Memorandum, FDR to Wayne Coy re: Aid to Russia, August 2, 1941, President's Secretary's Files: Diplomatic Correspondence: Russia, 1941 (Box 49). http://www.fdrlibrary.marist.edu/archives/significant-findingaid.html

Ferrell, Robert H. *Harry S. Truman: A Life.* Columbia: University of Missouri Press, 1994.

Ferrell, Robert H., Ed. *Dear Bess: The Letters from Harry to Bess Truman, 1910–1959.* Columbia: University of Missouri Press, 1983.

Fitch, James Marston. The Lawn: America's Greatest Architectural Achievement. *American Heritage Magazine*, Volume 35, Issue 4 (June/July 1984), pages 51, 53, and 55.

Gerson, Noel B. *TR: A Biographical Novel about Theodore Roosevelt.* New York: Doubleday and Company, 1970.

Gilbert, Martin. *Churchill: A Life.* New York: Henry Holt and Company, 1991.

Grant, James. *John Adams: Party of One.* New York: Farrar, Straus and Giroux, 2005.

Greenstein, Fred I. *Profiles of U.S. Presidents: Dwight D. Eisenhower.* www.presidentprofiles.com. Accessed 6/28/10.

Gettysburg Address. Abraham Lincoln Civil War Speech, Genesis of the Gettysburg Address. http://americancivilwar.com/north/lincoln.html#undergod, retrieved 8/23/12.

Herbert Hoover Presidential Library and Museum. The Published Writings of Herbert Hoover. *Public Papers of the Presidents of the United States: Herbert Hoover*, Volume 3: *1931*, and Volume 4: *1932-33*. Washington, DC: United States Government Printing Office, 1976.

Herbert Hoover Presidential Library and Museum. The Published Writings of Herbert Hoover. *The Memoirs of Herbert Hoover*, Volume 2: *The Cabinet and the Presidency 1920-1933*, and Volume 3: *The Great Depression 1929–1941.* New York: The Macmillan Company, 1952.

Hofstadter, Richard. *The American Political Tradition: And the Men Who Made It.* New York: Alfred A. Knopf, 1968.

Holy Bible, New International Version®, NIV® Copyright ©1973, 1978, 1984, 2011 by Biblica, Inc.

Hoover Institution, Stanford University, An American Friendship: Herbert Hoover and Poland, June 1, 2005 to August 1, 2005, library and archives » exhibits, http://www.hoover.org/library-and-archives/exhibits/27245. Retrieved 6/13/2013.

Keyes, Ralph. *The Wit and Wisdom of Harry Truman: A Treasury of Quotations, Anecdotes, and Observations.* New York: Gramercy Books, 1995.

Letter, Harry S. Truman to Herbert Hoover, May 24, 1945, formally inviting Hoover to the White House to meet Truman and discuss the food situation in Europe. Papers of Herbert Hoover: Post-Presidential Files-Individual. http://www.trumanlibrary.org/hoover/internaltemplate.php?tldate=1945-05-24&groupid=5101&collectionid=hoover

Letter from Jackie Robinson to President Dwight D. Eisenhower. White House Central Files Box 731, File: OF-142-A-3, Dwight D. Eisenhower Library, National Archives and Records Administration.

Letter from Roger Jones to President Eisenhower concerning the Federal-Aid Highway Construction Program, June 28, 1956.

Levering, Ralph (*The Cold War*). Yalta Plants Seeds of Cold War. http://www.realclearhistory.com/2012/02/04/yalta_plants_seeds_of_cold_war_1447.html, http://shs.westport.k12.ct.us/jwb/AP/ColdWar/Yalta.htm. http://www.si.edu, 2/28/2012, Collections: February 4, 2012,

Library of Congress: The Alfred Whital Stern Collection of Lincolniana [Letter to Joseph Hooker from Lincoln, January 26, 1863.] http://memory.loc.gov. Retrieved 11/6/2012.

Lillback, Peter A., and Newcomb, Jerry. USA: Providence Forum Press, 2006.

The Lincoln Log: A Daily Chronology of the Life of Abraham Lincoln. Abraham Lincoln to Horatio Seymour, 23 March 1863, *CW*, 6:145–46; Alexander J. Wall, *A Sketch of the Life of Horatio Seymour 1810-1886* (Lancaster, PA: Lancaster Press, 1929), 23-25. http://www.thelincolnlog.org/view/1863/3/23

Mankowski, Diana, and Jose, Raissa. *MBC Flashback*. The 70th Anniversary of FDR's Fireside Chats, March 12, 1933. The Museum of Broadcast Communications. http://www.museum.tv/exhibitionssection.php?page=79

Mayo, Bernard. *Jefferson Himself: The Personal Narrative of a Many-Sided American*. Charlottesville: The University Press of Virginia, 1984.

McCullough, David. *John Adams*. New York: Simon and Schuster, 2001.

McCullough, David. *Truman*. New York: Simon & Schuster, 1992.

McElvaine, Robert S. *The Depression and New Deal*. New York: Oxford University Press, 2000.

Memorandum of Conference with the President on 5/15/60, dated May 16, 1960 regarding U-2 and summit conference [DDE's Papers as President, DDE Diary Series, Box 50, Staff Notes May 1960 (1)].

Merriam-Webster Word Central, Student Dictionary. http://www.wordcentral.com/cgi-bin/student?book=Student&va=cold%20war. Retrieved 3/2/18.

Millard, Candice. *The River of Doubt: Theodore Roosevelt's Darkest Journey*. New York: Broadway Books, 2005.

Minutes of Cabinet Meeting on the Salk vaccine, April 29, 1955 [DDE's Papers as President, Cabinet Series, Box 5, Cabinet Meeting of 4/29/55].

Morgan, Edmund S. *The Genuine Article: A Historian Looks at Early America*. New York: W. W. Norton and Company, 2004.

Morris, Edmund. *Theodore Rex*. New York: The Modern Library, 2001.

Moskin, Robert J. *Mr. Truman's War: The Final Victories of WWII and the Birth of the Postwar World*. New York: Random House, 1996.

Padover, Saul K. *The Complete Jefferson*. New York: Duell, Sloan, and Pearce, Inc., 1943.

The Papers of George Washington: Documents - Introduction. Mary Katherine Goddard to George Washington. December 23, 1789, Baltimore http://gwpapers.virginia.edu/documents/goddard/index.html

Parker, Theodore. *Historic Americans*. Boston: Horace Fuller, 1878. http://www.archive.org/details/historicamerican00parkiala, contributed by University of California Libraries. Retrieved 1/05/12.

The Patriot Papers. Middle School, Spring 2003, Seattle http://si-pwebsrch02.si.edu/search?q=cache:aG1y3G5YFZUJ:http://georgewashington.si.edu/kids/pp4m_7.html+john%20adams&output=xml_no_dtd&client=www-si-edu&proxystylesheet=www-si-edu&site=si_all

Perkins, Frances. The Roosevelt I Knew, serial installment in *Collier's: The National Weekly* for August 24, 1946. http://www.oldmagazinearticles.com/new_deal_labor_secretary_francis_perkins_memory_of_FDR_pdf

Peterson, Merrill D. *Adams and Jefferson: A Revolutionary Dialogue.* Oxford: Oxford University Press, 1976.

Pinsker, Mathew. The Soldiers' Home. In *Abraham Lincoln: Great American Historians on Our Sixteenth President*, edited by Brian Lamb and Susan Swain. New York: PublicAffairs, 2008, pages 151–153.

The President's News Conference of July 28, 1949, pages 402–405, #166 of Public Papers of the President of the United States Harry S. Truman: Containing the Public Messages, Speeches, and Statements of the President, January 1 to December 31, 1949, Washington: United States Government Printing Office, 1964.

Reagan, Ronald. Address to the National Association of Evangelicals ("Evil Empire Speech"). Voices of Democracy: The U.S. Oratory Project. College Park: University of Maryland, March 8, 1983. Retrieved April 19, 2015.

Reeves, Richard. *President Reagan: The Triumph of Imagination.* New York: Simon & Schuster, 2005.

Report of the National Conservation Commission. February, 1909. Special message from the President of the United States transmitting a report of the National Conservation Commission, with accompanying papers, Image 10 of 279, page 4.

Ronald Reagan Presidential Library & Museum. Remarks on Receiving the Final Report of the Presidential Commission on the Space Shuttle Challenger Accident, June 9, 1986. http://www.reagan.utexas.edu/archives/speeches/publicpapers.html#.Uotyo2znbIU; http://www.reagan.utexas.edu/search/speeches/speech_srch.html, dtSearch Web Search. Retrieved 11/19/13.

The Ronald Reagan Presidential Foundation & Library. http://www.reaganfoundation.org/. Public Papers of Ronald Reagan, April 1985, Remarks Congratulating the Villanova University Wildcats on Winning the National Collegiate Athletic Association Basketball Championship, April 4, 1985. http://www.reagan.utexas.edu/archives/speeches/publicpapers.html#.UksCz2wo4dW; http://www.reagan.utexas.edu/archives/speeches/1985/40485a.htm.

The Ronald Reagan Presidential Foundation & Library. President Reagan's Domestic Policy: A More Perfect Union. http://www.reaganfoundation.org/the-presidency.aspx. Retrieved 11/15/2013.

The Ronald Reagan Presidential Foundation & Library. Reagan Quotes, Inaugural Address, 1/20/1981. http://www.reaganfoundation.org/the-presidency.aspx. Retrieved 11/15/2013.

The Ronald Reagan Presidential Foundation & Library. Reagan Quotes, News Conference, 1/29/1981. http://www.reaganfoundation.org/the-presidency.aspx. Retrieved 11/15/2013.

The Ronald Reagan Presidential Foundation and Library, Home, Ronald Reagan, White House Diary, Thursday, June 18, 1981. http://www.reaganfoundation.org/white-house-diary.aspx. Retrieved 6/18/2013.

The Ronald Reagan Presidential Foundation & Library, Public Papers of Ronald Reagan, August 1983. Joint Communique Following Discussions with President

Miguel de la Madrid Hurtado of Mexico, August 14, 1983. http://www.reagan.utexas.edu/archives/speeches/1983/81483e.htm; http://www.reaganfoundation.org/.

The Ronald Reagan Presidential Foundation & Library. REAGANFOUNDATION.ORG/WHITE-HOUSE-DIARY. http://www.reaganfoundation.org/WHITE-HOUSE-DIARY.aspx. October 12, 14, 25, and 31, 1981.

Russell, Thomas H. A. M., LL. D. Editor-in-Chief. *The Political Battle of 1912: Party Platforms, National Issues, Great Leaders*: Official Edition. L. h. Walter, 1912.

Sandburg, Carl. *Abraham Lincoln: The Prairie Years and the War Years*, One-Volume Edition, San Diego: A Harvest Book—Harcourt, Inc., 1982.

Shenk, Joshua Wolf. *Lincoln's Melancholy: How Depression Challenged a President and Fueled His Greatness.* Boston: Houghton Mifflin Company, 2005.

Siekierski, Maciej. History of a Friendship: Herbert Hoover and Poland; and Recalling the post-war relief efforts of the thirty-first president, in SIDEBAR to Remembering the Warsaw Uprising, *Hoover Digest* » 2004 no. 4, http://www.hoover.org/publications/hoover-digest/article/7495, October 30, 2004, retrieved 6/13/2013.

Simon, James F. *What Kind of Nation: Thomas Jefferson, John Marshall, and the Epic Struggle to Create a United States.* New York: Simon & Schuster, 2002.

Smith, Jean Edward. *John Marshall: Definer of a Nation.* New York: Henry Holt and Company, 1996.

Smith, Page. *John Adams,* Volume II: *1784–1826,* Garden City, NY: Doubleday & Company, Inc., 1962.

Stimson, Henry L., and Bundy, McGeorge. *On Active Service in Peace and War.*, New York: Harper and Brothers, 1948.

Strauss, Valerie. Why so many teachers leave—and how to get them to stay. *Washington Post*, June 12, 2015. https://www.washingtonpost.com/news/answer-sheet/wp/2015/06/12/why-so-many-teachers-leave-and-how-to-get-them-to-stay/. Retrieved 10/25/15.

Sydnor, Charles S. *Gentlemen Freeholders: Political Practices in Washington's Virginia.* Chapel Hill, NC, 1952.

Theodore Roosevelt, "The Strenuous Life" (10 April 1899). Leroy G. Dorsey, Texas A&M University, last updated July 11, 2007. http://archive.vod.umd.edu/internat/tr1899int.htm. Retrieved 12/18/2018.

Theodore Roosevelt Association. Speeches, Research/Resources on TR, The Strenuous Life. http://www.theodoreroosevelt.org/research/speech%20strenuous.htm. Retrieved 12/13/2012.

Thompson, Mary V. MVLA Publications, Research Historian, Mount Vernon Ladies' Association (2003-2010). QUOTES: George Washington's References to God and Religion, Together with Selected References to Death, Eternity, Charity, and Morality #457, page 87 (from GW to his old friend, Dr. David Stuart [the stepfather of Martha Washington's grandchildren], 6/15/1790, *The Writings of George Washington*, 31:53–54). http://www.mountvernon.org/educational-resources/library/digital-collections

Truman, Harry S. *Memoirs by Harry S. Truman*, Volume Two: *Years of Trial and Hope*. Garden City, New York: Doubleday & Company, 1956.

Watkins, T. H. *The Great Depression: America in the 1930s.* Boston: Little, Brown and Company, 1993.

Wilber, Del Quentin. *Rawhide Down: The Near Assassination of Ronald Reagan.* New York: Henry Holt and Company, 2011.

Wilentz, Sean. *The Age of Reagan: A History 1974–2008*. New York: HarperCollins Publishers, 2008.

Wilstach, Paul. *Patriots off Their Pedestals. Indianapolis:* The Bobbs-Merrill Company, 1927.

Wood, Gordon S. *The Radicalism of the American Revolution*. New York: Vintage Books, A Division of Random House, Inc., 1993.

Yockelson, Mitchell. "I Am Entitled to the Medal of Honor and I Want It": Theodore Roosevelt and His Quest for Glory. *Prologue Magazine*, Vol. 30, No. 1 (Spring 1998). http://www.archives.gov/publications/prologue/1998/spring/roosevelt-and-medal-of-honor-1.html

Zamoyski, Adam. *The Last King of Poland.* Great Britain: A Phoenix Giant Paperback, 1998.

www.ingramcontent.com/pod-product-compliance
Lightning Source LLC
Chambersburg PA
CBHW022016300426
44117CB00005B/215